WESTERN EUROPE AND JAPAN BETWEEN
THE SUPERPOWERS

WESTERN EUROPE & JAPAN BETWEEN THE SUPER POWERS

WOLF MENDL

CROOM HELM
London & Sydney

ST. MARTIN'S PRESS
New York

© 1984 Wolf Mendl
Croom Helm Ltd, Provident House, Burrell Row,
Beckenham, Kent BR3 1AT

Croom Helm Australia Pty Ltd, First Floor, 139 King Street,
Sydney, NSW 2001, Australia

British Library Cataloguing in Publication Data

Mendl, Wolf
    Western Europe and Japan between the superpowers.
    1. United States–Relations (Military) with
    Western European countries
    2. Western European countries–Relations
    (Military) with United States
    3. United States–Relations (Military) with
    Japan   4. Japan–Relations (Military)
    with United States
    I. Title
    335'.0335'073   E183.8.w/

ISBN 0-7099-1722-8

All rights reserved. For information, write:
St. Martin's Press, Inc., 175 Fifth Avenue, New York, NY 10010
First published in the United States of America in 1984

Library of Congress Card Catalog Number: 84-40047

ISBN 0-312-86401-9

Printed and bound in Great Britain

CONTENTS

List of Tables and Figures

Acknowledgements

Introduction	1
1. Security in a Changing International Environment	5
2. The Military Dimension	33
3. The Alliance with the United States	55
4. Relations with the Soviet Union	84
5. Europe, Japan and the Third World	114
6. Europe's and Japan's Choices	140
Glossary	166
Appendix I: The North Atlantic Treaty (1949)	168
Appendix II: Treaty of Mutual Cooperation and Security between the United States of America and Japan (1960)	172
Index	176

TABLES AND FIGURES

Tables

3.1	NATO and Warsaw Pact Ground and Air Forces in Place in Europe (Excluding the Territory of the USSR), July 1983	72
5.1	Production, Import and Export of Primary Energy	116
5.2	Principal Sources for the Import of Hard Coal, Crude Petroleum and Natural Gas in 1979	117
5.3	Domestic Mine Production of Non-ferrous Metals as Percentage of Consumption, 1980-1	120
5.4	Principal Sources for the Import of Non-ferrous Metals and of Ores	121

Figure

5.1	Japanese Energy Conservation	119

ACKNOWLEDGEMENTS

I am very grateful to Christoph Bertram for first encouraging me to write this book. Barrie Paskins read the initial draft and then the revised versions of several chapters, making invaluable and stimulating suggestions. I owe a great debt to David Thomas, who spent many hours collecting and collating the material for the tables in Chapter 5 and providing much additional information. My wife not only typed the whole manuscript, but kept a sharp eye on my style and expression. Finally, David Croom bore the long delays with noble patience. Without the constant encouragement and support of all those mentioned, I might never have completed this exercise. They bear no responsibility for the conclusions or for any shortcomings in the book.

INTRODUCTION

This essay is intended as a contribution to the current debate over the security of Western Europe and Japan. That debate is turning into a confrontation between those who want to convert two more-or-less self-contained alliances between the United States and its Western partners into a global alliance of the West under American leadership, and those who want to move away from the present system and pursue non-aligned or neutralist policies.

I find myself in the uncomfortable position of agreeing with some of the premises of both points of view. I believe that Western Europe and Japan require an association with the United States in order to counter potential pressures and threats from the Soviet Union. On the other hand, I am also convinced that the interests of Europe and Japan are not necessarily the same as those of the United States, and that Europeans and Japanese should coordinate their efforts to develop independent and constructive policies which would lay the foundations for a more peaceful world.

The course of world politics in the postwar era has been largely determined by the rival imperialisms of the two superpowers. American imperialism was dominant until the 1970s, and it was the objective of Soviet imperialism to catch up with it in military strength and political influence. The Russians have achieved this objective to a large extent and, as a consequence, superpower rivalry has entered a new phase, assuming a genuine global dimension.

The relationship between the United States and the Soviet Union is a complex and subtle one, involving elements of competition and co-operation. Western Europe and Japan are caught in the middle of their rivalry. If forced to choose between them, I am sure that most of us in the West would prefer to live in the shadow of American imperialism. Our life-style and personal and social values have more in common with those of the Americans than those of the Russians. The freedom and order of our societies, with all their deficiencies and imperfections, are preferable to the arbitrary power of a rigid bureaucracy, operating according to an exclusive orthodoxy, whose authority is buttressed by an ubiquitous secret police.

Nevertheless, we are also neighbours of the Soviet Union, and for the sake of our mutual survival we must learn to live in peace with our fellow human beings in Russia. Strangely, it is the complicated relationship of the two imperialisms which ensured that peace and our security over the past four decades. However, there are dangers as well as opportunities in the present conjuncture of events, which require a change of habits of thought as well as of policies if we are to survive this critical stage in world history.

The dangers are usually stressed, especially those of the nuclear arms race. While paying due regard to them, I have also sought to stress the opportunities that have arisen, precisely because of the impact of that arms race on the mutual relationship of the superpowers. Thus, for example, I have devoted only scant attention to the absorbing controversy over the modernization of Theatre Nuclear Forces (TNF) in Europe. By the time this book is in print, much of the argument may have been overtaken by events. The great debate will eventually subside, even if some Pershings and some cruise missiles are deployed, as seems most likely. There may be a few nasty moments, and perhaps an agreement will eventually be hammered out to moderate this particular element in the competition between the United States and the Soviet Union, but they and their allies will doubtlessly adjust, and we shall move forward up the spiral into the next phase of confrontation/co-operation which is the hallmark of contemporary superpower relations.

On the other hand, the long-term significance of the current issue of Intermediate-range Nuclear Forces (INF) does not lie in the balance of armaments but in its impact on the drive to build global alliance systems. The Russian insistence on including British and French nuclear forces in the total on the Western side, and the insistence of the Japanese that the INF negotiations should be conducted with a global perspective because some of Russia's SS-20s might be withdrawn to the east of the Urals in the event of an agreement in Europe, strengthen the argument of all those who believe that the security of the West is one and indivisible, and should therefore be cemented in an all-embracing alliance.

It is not the immediate perspective of the next few years which concerns me most, but the problem of relating the realities of today to the need of developing new concepts of what constitutes the 'national' interest in a rapidly changing environment. Quite apart from the natural diversity of interests between the United States and its friends, there are two factors which make it imperative that we try to look for fresh approaches and move away from the stark 'either/or' perspective that seems to dominate the current debate.

Introduction

The first affects the trend of the relations between the United States and the Soviet Union. If we take a long view, they are on a course which is very dangerous for the future of the world. The distinguishing features of the Soviet and, even more, the American 'empires' may bear little resemblance to those of empires in the past, but they display the same tendency of all empires to expand their spheres of influence and control. As there are only two contenders in the field, the risk of a head-on collision is great, especially if one of them should be tempted to think the time was ripe to make a dash for world dominion. In the past such rivalries were usually settled by war, or by the collapse of one party through decay and revolution.

Historically, those events were a wretched experience for many people, but they did not bring about universal disaster because large parts of the globe remained outside the range of empires and, however ferocious and destructive the conflict, men's capacity for destruction did not match their capacity for regeneration. If one centre of civilization collapsed as a result of such a clash, then others would take its place. This happened with Europe after the last great convulsion. It was finally dethroned from its pre-eminence in world politics, and its role as a pacemaker passed to the United States and Russia.

The unimaginable means of devastation at the disposal of the two giants and their ability to carry it into every corner of the world, make the prospect of a conflict between them quite horrifying; a view fortunately shared so far by their leaders as well as by everyone else. However, this awareness does not seem to have affected the traditional conceptual framework in which they conduct their policies. They are still engaged in a power struggle, preparing for a war which they agree would be folly but apparently assume to be the final arbiter of their competition – as it has always been in the past.

Such cognitive dissonance brings one to the second factor. The technological revolution through which we are living, especially the development of instant communication and control of information and the rapid movement of people and goods, is making the idea of the self-contained, sovereign nation-state, which periodically resorts to war to assert its rights and defend its interests, an outdated concept. Again, most statesmen and politicians, and even a few enlightened military men, would share this sentiment, but their policies hardly fit such a view. Moreover, nuclear armaments are being refined constantly to make them more credible for war-fighting, and they are no longer confined to the giants but are spreading to lesser powers, with all the risks that implies for the safety of the world.

This book is, therefore, something more than an academic study. It offers a broad historical analysis of the post-1945 era, and reflects on its implications for the future. It concludes with a discussion of the policy options facing Europe and Japan, and suggests the one that holds out the best hope for the future.

W.M.

September 1983

1 SECURITY IN A CHANGING INTERNATIONAL ENVIRONMENT

For nearly forty years Western Europe and Japan have enjoyed peace and prosperity within a remarkably stable environment. The full explanation of this state of affairs must be left to historians of future generations, but there can be little doubt that a major cause has been their geopolitical situation between the United States and the Soviet Union and the unique relationship between the two superpowers. Close ties with the United States have protected Western Europe and Japan against Soviet pressures, but this has not prevented them from developing economic and political relations with Russia, and from exercising a fair degree of autonomy in their foreign policies.

However, over the past ten years or so the foundations of the postwar world order have begun to crumble. The economic system, which rested on a stable monetary order and the availability of plentiful and cheap sources of energy and raw materials, and the political system, which rested on the military supremacy of the United States, are being undermined. It seems that the cosy relationship with the United States has gone for good, and that a changed international environment makes it both necessary and opportune that Western Europe and Japan should develop new directions in their external relations.

While there is widespread agreement that things are not what they used to be and that there is a need for readjustment, the debate about what should be done is essentially between those who want to revise or expand the old pattern of an American-led Western security system and those who are looking for radical alternatives in the form of neutralism or non-alignment. In this study I examine policies which would combine some of the features of the old system, which has worked so well in the past, with more radical approaches appropriate to a rapidly changing world; and it is precisely for that reason that I propose to link Japan with Europe.

Hitherto, discussions of the problems of Western security have concentrated either on the relations between Europe and the United States or on the bilateral security system between Japan and America. In recent years there has been a tendency to link the two regions in a kind of embryonic Western Alliance around the United States. The purpose of this book is to shift the focus away from an American-dominated alliance system to a more independent Euro-Japanese perspective.

In choosing to concentrate on the three major states of Western Europe (Britain, France and the German Federal Republic) and on Japan, I have been guided by the conviction that the features and interests that they have in common are more important than their obvious differences. All are advanced industrial democracies, in the forefront of what has been called the second industrial revolution. They have a unique geopolitical location at each end of the Soviet Empire. Although they may no longer be regarded as great powers in the traditional sense, they are still powers with 'general interests' which embrace the whole states-system and thus include the entire world.[1]

The Four States as 'Powers'

Britain, France, Germany and Japan certainly thought of themselves as great powers in the prewar period. Seen from the perspective of half a century later, it is evident that the first two were dominant powers in decline, and the other two great powers aspiring to dominance.[2]

All of them are still important actors in world politics today, although there was a considerable hiatus before Germany and Japan returned to the international stage. Three of the states had been formidable military powers, and the fourth, Britain, relied upon a navy which, until the First World War, was designed to be superior to the combined strength of any other two navies. All four had looked on military force as the ultimate sanction in the promotion of the national interest: economic, political, diplomatic or cultural instruments were deployed in the pursuit of national objectives on the understanding that if they failed, military action would either be threatened or taken in their support.

The events of the Second World War and the circumstances surrounding its conclusion confirmed Britain's self-image as one of the great powers of the world. Far-sighted men warned against the illusions of grandeur, and pointed to dramatic changes in the international environment which had reduced Britain's status at best to that of a second-class power.[3] But it took a very long time to adjust policy to the new realities, and then only in a piecemeal and haphazard fashion as a result of a series of painful shocks. British governments continued to act as if Britain were a great power of the first rank, and the country lived well beyond its economic and military means.

For France the War had been a humiliating experience. It had been defeated and occupied and had played only a secondary role in its liberation. But, regardless of the economic and social consequences of this devastating experience, postwar French governments, irrespective of their political complexion, were determined to recover its status as the pre-eminent power on the European continent, west of the Elbe, and as a great power with a worldwide empire. All this seemed possible because, in spite of its wartime history, France had emerged as a member of the victorious alliance.

Not so Germany and Japan; they had lost control over the management of their affairs, and for a few years Germany ceased to exist as a state. The postwar leaders had no thought of great-power status for their countries. Their business was to ensure national survival, which perforce meant concentrating on economic recovery and, once their formal independence had been restored, this was the only area of policy in which they could achieve international importance. The fortuitous combination of their defeat and destruction with the removal of the customary preoccupations of a great power – an expansive foreign policy backed by expensive military and other means – enabled Germany and Japan to restructure and modernize their economies under particularly favourable international conditions: security ensured by the *Pax Americana* and the stability of the international financial regime set up by the Bretton Woods Agreement, combined with the availability of plentiful and cheap raw materials.

In the late 1960s the prosperity and economic strength of the two countries had made them states with general interests. But if one were to regard them as great powers, then they were powers with a difference in that they lacked military strength commensurate with their global economic interests. Awareness of being a 'power' and the aspiration to play a 'role' began to emerge at this time. In Japan it took the form of conscious competition in the economic league table, with success measured by rates of growth and size of Gross National Product (GNP). In Germany it took the form of a renewed awareness of its central importance in Europe, which found expression in the *Ostpolitik*.

In the 1970s all four states could claim that they were powers of world importance. Britain and France possessed nuclear weapons and were permanent members of the United Nations Security Council; all four were members of the economic summit club of the leading industrialized countries. Until recently, at least, they were the only states in the second rank after the United States and the Soviet Union. This claim is no longer unambiguous today: other states or groups of states are emerging to challenge their unique status.

At present, then, the four states which are the subject of this study may be said to occupy positions as major powers in the global system, if we accept the definition of general interest as that which distinguishes them from lesser powers, even though they may not possess some of the conventional attributes of power. They have one other feature in common which enhances their global importance: they are advanced industrial and technological societies with highly developed and flexible social and political structures. These characteristics may enable them to adjust to a rapidly changing environment and to retain their dynamism.

One indication of their ability to adjust is the trend towards replacing the three separate major states in Western Europe with a new 'power', including a number of smaller states as well, whose combined resources would make it the world's second economic giant, after the USA and ahead of Japan. The significance of the European Economic Community (EEC) as a new power centre and its relationship with Japan will be discussed later in this chapter and throughout the book, but if The Organization of Petroleum Exporting Countries (OPEC) is to be regarded as a 'power' that has a far-reaching impact on the international system, there is even more reason to think of EEC as a potential challenge to the old order. Unlike OPEC, which has no political, geographic or cultural cohesion, EEC has all of these, and might become a link between the old world-order based on the primacy of the nation state and the emergence of a new pattern of multistate groupings in the international system.

Changing Patterns in the International System

The first of three distinctive postwar periods began shortly after the end of the Second World War in 1945. This was the period of the Cold War, dominated by the antagonism of the United States and the Soviet Union. In spite of initial Soviet advances, it was not a contest of equals. The United States was militarily and economically the dominant world power. Its policy of containing Soviet expansion was buttressed by a series of separate alliances which were constructed on the peripheries of the Soviet Empire in the late 1940s and the first half of the 1950s. Although it exercised some ideological influence in the world, Russia's real power was confined to its borders in the Eurasian landmass.

Security in a Changing International Environment

The Cold War period gradually gave way in the mid-1950s to a period of mixed relaxation and tension in the relations between the two giants. The emergence of Russia as a nuclear power after its first test explosion in 1949 gave some semblance of equality to the United States and the Soviet Union, and set them apart from all the other members of the international system, although for many years Russia was not able to project its conventional military power far from its borders. The middle years of the decade of the 1950s saw the first stirrings of an attempt at joint management of world affairs with the ending of hostilities in Korea, Eisenhower's 'open skies' proposals, 'Atoms for Peace', the establishment of the International Atomic Energy Agency in 1956, and the beginning of a series of occasional summit meetings.

Severe tensions continued, however, to punctuate the efforts at finding a mutual accommodation. They included the two crises of 1955 and 1958 in the Strait of Taiwan, periodic crises over Berlin, the U-2 incident which broke up the Paris summit of 1960, and most important, the Cuban missile crisis of October 1962. The mixture of confrontation and co-operation in the superpower relationship was the result not only of American perceptions of a basic nuclear 'equality' – especially after the launching of Sputnik in 1957 – and of Khrushchev's domestic policies, but also of the decline of each power's hegemony in its respective camp.

Each faced rebellious allies: the Americans with de Gaulle after 1958 and the Russians with China. When the Sino-Soviet conflict went 'public' in 1961, it was a damaging and lasting blow to the Soviet Union's domination of the world communist movement. But even before it became apparent that neither superpower was in full command of its alliances, there had been opposition to their domination of the world scene. The Afro-Asian non-aligned movement led by Nehru, Nasser and Sukarno, and encouraged by Zhou Enlai, was a protest against the spread of Cold War politics throughout the world.

The movement towards a multipolar or polycentric world order gathered momentum in the 1960s, and was the consequence of many factors. It culminated in the late 1960s and early 1970s, which were the heyday of the period of détente. The series of arms-control negotiations and agreements and the care with which the two superpowers avoided direct confrontation, did not, however, obliterate the fundamental antagonism between them.

The third historical period witnessed a resurfacing of open hostility. It began in the late 1970s and was, again, the consequence of many and complex influences. The emphasis is once more on rivalry rather than co-operation, but it is not a simple return to the Cold War period. For one thing, the element of collaboration between the superpowers has not disappeared completely; for another, they operate in a world which is very different from the world of the early postwar years. Many factors in their mutual relationship have changed, and so has the international environment.

It is to this context that Western Europe and Japan must adjust, and it would be foolish of them to try to resurrect the patterns of the past. Instead, new and bold visions of the world-order are necessary to take into account new circumstances and to increase the prospects of international peace.

One of the main difficulties of a study such as this is to fix on an appropriate time-scale. If we make it too short and concentrate on the immediate present, then much of the discussion will look distinctly odd in a few years' time when the Reagan Administration may be no more, and the government of Chancellor Schmidt may have been replaced by a government dominated by the conservative CDU/CSU.[4] Nor is it inconceivable that there may be a new period of relaxation in the relationship of the superpowers in the latter half of the 1980s. On the other hand, a long-term view, perhaps towards the end of the century and beyond, is bound to be very fuzzy and vague, dominated by so many imponderables and qualifications as to become meaningless.

For example, important new actors may have appeared on the world stage, helping to create new patterns and perspectives in international politics. Thus, even today China is often bracketed with the two superpowers, either as one of their kind or as nearest to them, and people talk about 'the three superpowers'. This view is based entirely on China's potential, but has no foundation in present-day reality nor in any realistic prospects for the next decade or two. China is a developing country plagued with enormous economic, social and political problems. Apart from its small but growing nuclear armament, it does not have the capacity to project its military force far beyond the border regions. Its general interests are symbolized by permanent membership of the Security Council, but its impact on the world remains platonic rather than material.[5] Above all, it is still not certain whether the present government will be able to stabilize and effectively manage this vast country with more than a thousand million inhabitants.

A quite different challenge to the position of the industrialized states in the world order comes from the cartel of oil producing countries grouped in OPEC. While they lack any kind of cohesion, other than in the fixing of prices and then only after bitter wrangling among themselves, and cannot be fitted into the hierarchy of powers, their ability to influence the course of events in the world cannot be denied. They may be regarded alongside the great multi-national corporations as exercising new forms of power without its traditional trappings and geographical base, but with general interests and an impact comparable to those of a conventional great power.

Elsewhere, one can perceive the emergence of new regional giants, such as Brazil, Nigeria and India. Their power potential is based on physical size, population, and resources. But even more than China, they are still over the horizon. The Nigerian government, for instance, has proclaimed an ambitious foreign policy which is directed towards establishing a *Pax Nigeriana*, resting on its dominance of West Africa as the largest and wealthiest state in the region and on its claim to leadership in the struggle against the white-minority regime of South Africa. But these aspirations depend for their fulfilment on the government's ability to develop and harness Nigeria's resources for this purpose. Nigeria's problem is illustrative of the problems facing other would-be great powers: the vision of national grandeur is an essential element in creating a sense of nationhood among its people, but it cannot be made real unless solid social, economic and political foundations are laid first.[6]

The problem of finding the right time-scale is compounded by the dangers of accepting a particular pattern of events as more or less immutable. The pattern may be one of the inevitable cycle of revolution alternating with periods of stability, or of the inevitability of power struggles within a permanent system consisting of competing sovereign states.[7] Thus, it is possible to see an indefinite continuation of superpower rivalry which dominates the world in alternating periods of tension and relaxation. The Cold War was followed by a relaxation of tensions in the mid-1950s, to be followed by a period of tension from 1958 to 1962. Then came détente from the mid-1960s until 1977, to be followed by renewed tension and an accelerated arms race. According to this pattern, another period of relaxation is due to follow, and the only question is, When?

To avoid the straitjacket of historical determinism and to get around the problem of the right time-scale when discussing the options and policies of Western Europe and Japan, I propose to look at the dynamics of the superpower relationship, which may enable us to consider alternatives other than a mere acceptance of the need to adjust to the apparently interminable cycle of confrontation and détente in their relations.

How the Superpower System Works

The usual description of the United States and the Soviet Union is to call them 'superpowers'. Some scholars have challenged the term, arguing that there is no justification for identifying yet another species of power which would only obfuscate the already well-established classifications of power status. They would deny that the possession of massive nuclear arsenals justifies conferring such a status on the United States and the Soviet Union.[8]

They behave in the way great powers have always behaved. Because of their size, resources and capabilities they have become the dominant powers in the world, and have established a 'simple' or bipolar balance of power in contrast to the 'complex' or multipolar balance of several states, which existed before the war.[9] Their continental size is nothing new in history. The Roman Empire at its greatest extent, and ancient China were also states of enormous size which dominated the world around them. A 'simple' balance of power could also be said to have existed between the Roman and Persian Empires. The only reason for introducing a new category into the international system would be the existence of a new attribute of power which has hitherto been absent in history.

The novelty of American and Soviet power is the possession of a range of weapons systems which provides them with the capacity for mutual annihilation and the total destruction of any other state or group of states without fear of suffering a similar fate by way of preemptive attack or reprisal from these lesser states. As a result and in spite of the asymmetry of their respective geo-strategic situations, ideologies, social systems and forms of government, the United States and the Soviet Union have entered into a unique relationship that overarches the international system — a relationship that is a mixture of competition for world hegemony and a reluctant co-operation to ward off the catastrophe of a full-scale war between them as well as any challenge to their unique status as 'superpowers'. At one and the same time there exists a simple balance of power between them, and they exercise a kind of hegemony or domination over the rest of the world.[10]

Both sides are anxious if not determined to avoid a direct conflict which would have incalculable consequences for their own societies; this,

Security in a Changing International Environment

in spite of different concepts of deterrence and strategic doctrines.

Deterrence is a concept as old as the institution of war. It was expressed in the Latin aphorism *Si vis pacem, para bellum*,[11] and is the standard argument of the non-pacifist in his debate with the pacifist, reinforced by the belief that since there has always been war in the history of mankind there will always be war. These two articles of faith represent the traditional view of deterrence: only one's military strength will deter potential adversaries and thus keep the peace, but sooner or later war is inevitable either because one has lowered one's guard or because one party to a dispute believes it can attain its objectives by force of arms, or makes some grievous miscalculation to that effect.

For the first two decades of the nuclear age deterrence acquired a new meaning: the mutual deterrence of the nuclear powers which made war between them *unthinkable* as an instrument of policy. No one knows what a war between nuclear-armed states would be like. The indiscriminate nature of the weapons, the potential scale of their destructive powers, and their long-term effect through radiation make the conduct of war between two more-or-less equally armed states irrational. Hence the paradox that peace is preserved by the threat of irrational behaviour.

American deterrence theory, in the days when the US had an overwhelming superiority in nuclear weapons, was originally separated from concepts of military defence, and was based on the threat of the enemy's assured destruction. The Russians, whose strategic thinkers were not civilian academics coming from a variety of disciplines but professional military men, have taken a traditional view of deterrence. The military man relates the ability to deter to the ability to fight a war successfully. The object is to persuade the would-be adversary that an attack would lead to a conflict which one has the will and capability to win or, at least, which the opponent has no chance of winning. No distinction is made between deterrence and defence.[12] However, in practice the Soviet Union behaved as if it had understood and accepted the American concept of mutual deterrence, and during the Khrushchev era paid lip-service to it.

These differences in approach have their explanations in the historical experience of the two countries and their ideological preconceptions, but it does not mean that the Russians are any more willing to risk an armed conflict with the Americans. Prudence and a reliance on overwhelming superiority are the hallmarks of Soviet military thinking. The latter has so far been denied them in the nuclear field, and it is doubtful whether they will ever be able to achieve it. It is different in the conventional field, where they might be prepared to take risks in some regions on the assumption that the Americans would not dare to introduce the nuclear dimension into a conflict.

During the last thirty-five years of their rivalry, the superpowers have therefore avoided the kind of direct military confrontation which has so often been the outcome of contests for hegemony in the past. The nearest they came to the brink of war was during the Cuba missile crisis of 1962. What made this event particularly threatening was not only their direct confrontation in a very sensitive region for American security, but that the confrontation was over nuclear weapons.

The Cuba crisis was a turning point in their mutual relationship for a variety of reasons. It was a textbook example of crisis management, whose aim is to achieve a diplomatic victory without recourse to war.[13] On the other hand, it marked the beginning of the long road to the Soviet achievement of a rough nuclear strategic parity with the United States and the gradual acceptance of this fact by the Americans. The subsequent two decades were dominated by protracted bilateral arms-control negotiations, culminating in the two SALT (Strategic Arms Limitation Talks) agreements and the limited anti-ballistic missile (ABM) deployment agreement of 1972.

Until now, at least, the superpowers have also had a tacit understanding to keep nuclear weapons out of their rivalry for influence over third countries and to prevent the spread of such weapons to other powers; one of the objectives behind the Partial Test Ban Treaty of 1963 and *the* objective of the Non-Proliferation Treaty (NPT) of 1968.

This recognition of the desirable limits to their competition, often described as a 'limited adversary relationship', gradually led to a pattern in world politics known as 'détente'. Beginning in the mid-1960s, it flowered in the 1970s. The rivalry did not, however, disappear, nor was it necessarily relegated to second place in superpower policies. It was merely continued with due caution because neither side believed it could replace their joint hegemony with its own hegemony, judging it better to have half a loaf than no loaf at all. The Russians justified this state of affairs to themselves as a tactical ploy on the basis of their faith in the historically determined triumph of their social and political system. The Americans did so on the basis of their faith in the innate superiority of their social and political system, reiterated by President Reagan in his Inaugural Address,[14] and the conviction that the Soviet Union must either recognize this fact and adapt accordingly or eventually collapse internally through the strain of competition.

One of the examples of this restrained competition in practice has been superpower behaviour in the Middle East. The Johnson-Kosygin meeting at Glassboro established some ground rules for their rivalry in the region after the Six Days' War in 1967, whose implementation was to be facilitated by the Washington-Moscow Hot Line. The agreement did not prevent the Russians from building up Egypt militarily and giving it the means with which to launch the 'War of Attrition' (1969-70), while making sure that Egypt did not embark upon military adventures which might escalate into a superpower confrontation.

The Yom Kippur War in 1973 again seemed to bring the superpowers on to a collision course when the Soviet Union threatened to comply unilaterally with Egypt's request for a joint American-Russian force to supervise the Israeli withdrawal, and the United States responded by placing its forces on full alert throughout the world. Within hours the Russians had backed down and agreed to the despatch of a UN Emergency Force without troops from the five permanent members of the UN Security Council.

Once more it was evident that there were limits to Soviet-American competition. However, Egypt's subsequent move into the Western camp, the American diplomacy aimed at freezing the Soviet Union out of the Egyptian-Israeli peace settlement, and Russia's wooing of Syria and infiltration in the southern tip of the Arabian peninsula and Ethiopia, illustrated the determination of each to pursue its advantage at the expense of the other.

This pattern of interaction was noticeable in other parts of the world, and in the 1970s the Russians appeared to be pushing forward more aggressively, especially in Africa, taking advantage of the disarray in America over Vietnam and its aftermath. It is an oversimplification, however, to point only to Soviet activities in Angola and the Horn of Africa, and to overlook the American *rapprochment* with China, which was surely a very grave setback for the Soviet Union.

Seen from the perspectives of Moscow and Washington, superpower rivalry has taken the form of securing bases and the stationing of garrisons at strategic points; the gift or sale of arms and military technology; showing the flag by sending naval units on visits to ports and conducting regular exercises in the world's oceans, subverting governments friendly to the other superpower, and fighting wars by proxy through allies. In the use of all these methods, except arms transfers, it seems at first glance that the Soviet Union has made the more striking advances in the past decade. They reflect a greater Soviet ability to project military strength into all parts of the world and underline the fact that the main focus of superpower rivalry has shifted from the border regions of the Soviet Union in Europe. To paint, as a consequence, a picture of a threatening Soviet advance to world hegemony is, however, a distortion of the true state of affairs. The very success of the expansion of Russian influence has created new problems for the Soviet Union which I shall discuss more fully in the chapter on the Third World.

At the beginning of the 1980s, the strategic capabilities of the superpowers are at par. This fact alone suggests that there should be a greater stability in their mutual relationship: an increased caution in their competition, conducted within implicitly defined and tacitly agreed rules of conduct. It also points to a shared interest in keeping the world in some sort of order; above all, in preventing a challenge to their own supremacy. These tendencies first became apparent in the Nixon-Brezhnev agreement on 'Basic Principles of US-Soviet Relations', signed on 29 May 1972.[15]

On the other hand, as their rivalry began to sharpen at the end of the 1970s, there were indications that both the United States and Russia are trying to create two global alliance systems. The tendency is most noticeable in the American camp, where strategic thinking is dominated by visions of a US/West European/Sino-Japanese/ASEAN/ Australasian line-up to contain Soviet power. However, the Russians are playing the same game by establishing outposts throughout the world, and the so far unsuccessful attempt to give the Warsaw Pact a global dimension.[16]

There is also justification for thinking that some aspects of the superpower relationship, which have been characteristic of the past two decades or so, are on the decline. The reason for this stems partly from the continued contradiction between shared and conflicting interests and, more importantly, from developments that apparently escape their control or influence.

Their nuclear policies are failing. Arms control negotiations and agreements have not stabilized the bilateral arms race which is once again accelerating. Apart from the truism about the dynamics of technological development, fuelled by the conviction that neither side can afford to risk a break-through by the other, the asymmetry of perceptions means that neither party is convinced that it really wants *parity*. In spite of the doctrine of mutual assured destruction, the United States has always been accustomed to link its deterrent capability to qualitative though not necessarily quantitative superiority. The Soviet Union, on the other hand, with its military-dominated strategic think-

Security in a Changing International Environment

ing cannot conceive of security except in terms of military superiority.

Another and possibly more sinister reason for the weakening of mutural deterrence lies in the development of many different types of nuclear arms by both sides. The multiplication and sophistication of nuclear weapons at all levels of military activity, from shells and mines for use on the battlefield — barely distinguishable from conventional explosives in size and the radius of their impact — to horrific weapons of mass destruction, with all the stages of tactical, medium range, theatre and intermediate-range weapons in between, has undermined the distinction between *nuclear* deterrence and *traditional* deterrence.

Moreover, there had always been some in the West, especially in the United States, who insisted that deterrence would not be credible unless it was tied to a nuclear war-fighting capability. One of the earliest proponents of these ideas was Herman Kahn with his books on thermonuclear war and on escalation.[17] With the development of a great variety of nuclear weapons on both sides there came a much greater elaboration of doctrines for their use, leading to the strategy of flexible targeting.[18] Nuclear weapons have now become 'respectable' instruments of war. They are targeted on the opponent's command, control and communications (C3) network, on his troop concentrations, on his bases, airfields, railheads, and so on.

All this is done for the purpose of reinforcing deterrence, so we are told. The very prospect of the use of nuclear weapons on the battlefield will deter an opponent from contemplating even the smallest aggression. And, should there be a miscalculation or accident, then limited nuclear strikes will force the opponent to pause and reflect before descending into the madness of large-scale nuclear conflict. That may be so, and it is perfectly true that no nuclear weapon has been fired in war since 1945. Yet the optimism seems misplaced, especially among those who prepare for war precisely because 'there have always been wars'.

It could be that mankind is on the eve of a wholly new era in its history in which the use of war as an instrument of policy will be increasingly circumscribed so that it shall eventually be seen as an anachronism. We cannot be sure, however, and the current tendency to make nuclear warfare more and more credible could become a self-fulfilling prophecy.

The impact of these developments on the fundamental contradiction between the power rivalry of the United States and the Soviet Union and their shared interests becomes apparent in the contemporary *impasse* in arms control negotiations, making it necessary to develop a new conceptual framework to revive the process.[19] But it is not only on the bilateral level that progress seems to have come to a standstill. The policy to enforce the non-proliferation regime, the most spectacular example of Soviet-American collaboration, has also failed.

Over the last decade a nuclear weapons potential has spread to many countries as a result of the export of plants and technology by the industrialized countries and the general dissemination of scientific and technological knowledge. Able and skilled scientists, technicians and engineers can make simple nuclear devices on the basis of a careful study of published materials. French assistance to Israel in building the reactor at Dimona undoubtedly helped to bring that country to the threshold of a nuclear weapons capability. Similarly, the Canadians unwittingly assisted India towards its first nuclear explosion. Despite Japan's dependence on the United States for the supply of enriched uranium and the safeguards negotiated by the United States over the nuclear-fuel recycling plant, Japan has acquired the complete nuclear-fuel cycle and thus a potential weapons-production capability.

The state of a country's civilian nuclear-power generation may be only a very crude measure of its military nuclear potential, but it is noteworthy that among the nineteen leading producers in 1980, according to the *UN Yearbook of World Energy Statistics*, one finds not only Japan (second in output) and the German Federal Republic (fifth), but also such states as the Republic of Korea, India, Argentina and Pakistan, all of which are assumed either to have or to be interested in acquiring nuclear weapons. Israel and South Africa, both of which are suspected of having or about to have nuclear arms, are not even among the nineteen.

The existence of two small but independent nuclear arsenals in France and China has further complicated matters for the superpowers. In theory, Britain is a third independent nuclear power, but in practice the British deterrent is only semi-detached. France and China pose the problem of independent centres of nuclear decision-making for the Russians, adding to the uncertainties in their strategic analysis. They pose another kind of problem for the Americans: their 'independence' weakens the position of the United States as the leader of a global alliance system aimed at balancing and containing Soviet power.

The failure of the superpowers to make the world safe for their domination and to establish their undisputed credentials to be the managers of the international order, is partly due to their inability to prevent horizontal nuclear proliferation. Another reason is the immobilism resulting from their inhibited mutual relationship. This has encouraged assertions of independence from lesser powers allied to one or other superpower. The causes have been complex and peculiar in each case, but in all the moves were justified on the grounds of opposition to hegemonism. For the Chinese the moment of truth came over the crisis in the Strait of Taiwan when Khrushchev hesitated to support them against the Americans. French opposition to hegemonism goes back to the Yalta Conference from which they were excluded. The Yugoslavs and Romanians have refused unconditional membership in an ideological (in the case of Yugoslavia) and politico-military bloc (in the case of Romania).

In the Third World the superpowers have also been unable to impose their will in spite of, or perhaps because of, their overwhelming military resources. Clients for arms and economic assistance have escaped control, whether because of the existence of an alternative source of support (as in the case of Egypt after 1973), or as a result of domestic revolution (as in the case of Iran in 1979), or because of regional conflict (as in the case of Somalia in 1977). In all these and other instances each superpower has been a helpless spectator of the course of events. In their more immediate neighbourhoods they have occasionally asserted their interests ruthlessly and with effect, such as the American-inspired overthrow of the government of Arbenz in Guatemala (1954) and armed intervention in the Dominican Republic in 1965, and the Russian subjection of Hungary in 1956 and Czechoslovakia in 1968. The most recent examples are the Russian intervention in Afghanistan and American intervention in El Salvador.

Europe and Japan in the Superpower Balance

The pattern of the superpower system as revealed by its dynamics consists of two basic elements: unceasing competition and unwilling co-operation. The competition has the explicit (Soviet) or implicit (American) objective of world domination. The Russian objective is founded on a belief that the Soviet Union is in the vanguard of an inevitable historical process which will eventually encompass the whole world. The American objective is based on the belief that the principles which govern American society offer the best hope for human progress. There are, of course, many different ideological positions within each camp, and beneath the moralistic and ideological rhetoric both sides act according to their perception of the immediate national interest rather than the dictates of political ideology. None the less, they are agreed that their size, resources and, most important, their military strength should command universal acceptance of their leadership in world affairs. In their eyes all international problems are subordinate to their rivalry.

What gives their relationship a novel aspect, one which has been absent from the clash of other imperialist powers in the past, is their extreme reluctance to engage in direct conflict and, as a consequence, their readiness to engage in a form of limited co-operation to manage world affairs. This is the direct result of the means of destruction at their disposal which distinguish a superpower from all other powers and have made a nonsense of war between them — the traditional method of resolving contests for domination. The constant refinement of nuclear weapons and the never-ending introduction of new technologies of war cannot disguise the awareness on both sides that once they are engaged in direct combat and the first nuclear weapon has been used, however small and precise it might be, they are engaged on a road which could end in either cataclysmic destruction or abject surrender. To avoid the risk of having to make such a choice, they are driven to develop other means and to find new ways in which to conduct their conflict. It is paradoxical that in doing so they engage in a spiralling competition of piling up more and more weapons of mass destruction.

Future generations may look back upon our age as the beginning of a turning-point in human affairs when the military dimension began to decline in importance. The major states of Western Europe and Japan have a special part to play in such a development, precisely because their importance and influence in the world does not rest primarily on the military instruments at their disposal.

The superpower system provides them with a freedom of manoeuvre and the chance to influence the course of events away from the pattern of international relations which was established with the emergence of the European states system in the seventeenth century — a pattern dominated by a concept of the 'balance of power' which is periodically readjusted by diplomacy or war.[20] The opportunity to develop new structures has to be examined in the context of their relationships with the superpowers, with the rest of the world, and with each other.

Western Europe and Japan are integrated in the superpower balance on the side of the United States, but for a variety of reasons their outlook and interests are by no means identical with those of the United States.

A historical and cultural nexus links Europeans to Americans and Russians. The ties with Russia vary from country to country, but in the last analysis Russians think of themselves as Europeans as much as Frenchmen and Germans, so that it was not absurd for de Gaulle to talk of a Europe from the Atlantic to the Urals. However, although America may be separated from Europe by three thousand miles of water, the links between Europeans and Americans in every field of human endeavour have been much closer than those between the Russians and other Europeans, except for a tiny elite in eighteenth and nineteenth-century czarist Russia, many of whom were of non-Russian origin. It is, therefore, difficult to imagine that a political chasm such as exists today between Western Europe and the Soviet Union, could divide the two sides of the Atlantic.

Historically, such cultural connections have been absent in the case of Japan. Americans, Russians and Europeans were outsiders intruding into the East Asian region. Over the past thirty-five years exceptionally close ties have developed with the United States, but they are based essentially on many shared interests rather than on cultural affinities. Notwithstanding a widespread familiarity with the American way of doing things and of thinking, the Japanese feel a greater emotional affinity with the Chinese, which does not mean that they like them more. It maybe, however, that cultural differences will become less and less important relative to the increasingly shared life-styles, patterns of behaviour and values of Japanese, Americans and Europeans as they move into the post-industrial age.

The postwar scene in Europe has been dominated by a bipolar confrontation of two alliance systems facing each other across a clearly marked divide. Each alliance is led by a superpower which dominates a more-or-less integrated military structure. Though outwardly very similar, the alliances serve rather different purposes. The Atlantic Alliance exists to provide the West European states with American protection, while the Warsaw Pact exists to provide the Soviet Union with protection.

In the place of two multilateral alliances, there is a multipower structure in East Asia. At one level there is a triangular American-Soviet-Chinese relationship. At another level there are the regional sub-groupings of the Association of South-east Asian Nations (ASEAN) and the Vietnam-dominated states of Indochina. The members of ASEAN are linked to the United States, China and Japan in a variety of ways, and Vietnam has a formal treaty relationship with the Soviet Union, though it would be a rash person who suggests that this makes Vietnam a Soviet satellite. Finally, there is yet another level on which a stark confrontation exists between the two halves of the Korean peninsula.

Here all the four major powers of the region, including Japan, are involved, but the line-up behind the two Korean states is not unequivocal.

Moreover, whereas the European states are enmeshed in the problems and promises of West European integration, trying to evolve coordinated foreign policies in spite of conflicting interests and trying to come to terms with the requirements of the overlapping trans-Atlantic Alliance, Japan operates within a strictly circumscribed bilateral reltionship for which it has only a limited liability.

In spite of such differences, all four states have security relationships with the United States which seem to differ in several respects from the *ad hoc* and often short-lived alliances among powers in the past. First, they have lasted for more than thirty years and can continue indefinitely, without any formal time limit written into the treaties apart from provisions for review after a period of years which have now been passed. Secondly, there are clear geographical limitations written into the treaties, outside of which there is no formal obligation on the parties to assist each other. Thirdly, there is provision for some form of peace-time integration of the armed forces of the members and their stationing in allied territories. Finally, whether explicitly or implicitly, the security relationship is unique in the sense that Europeans and Japanese are quite clearly the junior partners, dependent in the last resort on American protection.

The other feature of their shared security problems is an adversary relationship with the Soviet Union. Its roots are geopolitical, historic and ideological. Moreover, the West European states and Japan are situated at the extremities of the Soviet Empire and in close proximity to its principal military forces.

The nature of the Soviet 'threat' is the subject of such emotional and partisan debate in the Western countries that it is almost impossible to form an objective judgement. The extreme secretiveness and security consciousness of the Russians make it very difficult, even with the help of satellites and the latest electronic sensors, to be sure of factual accuracy about the strength and deployment of their military forces. It is not impossible, however, to establish a generally reliable analysis of the strength, equipment and tactical doctrines of the Soviet armed forces.[21]

The task of objective assessment becomes still more difficult when one tries to link factual data with intentions. Soviet policy-making runs on a closed circuit, and little is known — and usually too late to be of much practical use — about the debates and power relationships among the leadership groups. When information does become available, either through defectors or, more commonly, through a painstaking analysis of official statements and the press, the significance attached to the information is often heavily coloured by preconceptions and psychological and emotional attitudes towards the Soviet Union.[22]

As far as Western Europe and Japan are concerned, the problem of assessment is complicated by the fact that their military dispositions are tied to those of the United States. If one were to remove the cover provided by the American TNF and conventional forces stationed in the European and East Asian regions, the Soviet Union would have an overwhelming superiority, especially in nuclear weapons. Those who advocate the removal of the American presence from Europe or Japan must first accept this simple fact.

It is, of course, a much more complicated matter than that and cannot be resolved by adding and subtracting figures. For instance, they tell us nothing about the training, technical performance and morale of the Russian forces. Moreover, Soviet military efficiency in Europe depends on the ability to control the East European states and to ensure their support in a crisis. Again, China is a crucial factor in the assessment of the military balance in East Asia, where the major portion of Soviet military strength is concentrated on the Sino-Soviet border.

Given the predominantly European orientation of the Soviet Union, the main concentration of Russian military power is in that region. In East Asia, on the other hand, the Soviet Union is on the defensive. Apart from being very far from their main centres of population and industry, the Russians face several security problems. They include a vague but deeply rooted perception of a 'Chinese menace' which, in its military dimension, includes the threatened isolation of the maritime province facing the Pacific Ocean, with its string of bases and industrial installations, by cutting the communications with western Siberia and European Russia. There is also the threat of a Japanese-American blockade of the Soviet Pacific fleet in the Seas of Japan and Okhotsk, a threat which became more serious as a result of the Egyptian-Israeli peace process and Egypt's swing into the Western camp, thus making access to the Indian Ocean region from the western end via the Mediterranean and the Red Sea more problematic. Finally, the Russians have always been haunted by the nightmare of a war on two fronts, of which the eastern front would be the more vulnerable from the point of view of geography and the ability to reinforce it.

Leaving aside the difficulties of gauging Soviet capabilities and intentions and the Russians' own security problems, the *prima facie* evidence of Soviet conventional strength in Europe and East Asia suggests that without the American guarantee, Western Europe and Japan would be justified in feeling threatened. This does not take into account Soviet nuclear armament which would leave Japan completely exposed without American protection, and faces only very limited nuclear forces in France and Britain. Enough has been said, therefore, to explain why in purely military terms the European powers and Japan cannot contemplate facing the Soviet Union without some sort of security arrangements involving the United States.

European and Japanese perceptions of the Soviet Union are not, however, identical to American perceptions. The differences are not confined to geographical factors nor to a different order of scale. They arise from the interest of developing economic relations with Russia in which the element of complementarity plays a large part. This interest is reinforced by the fact that Europeans and Japanese are neighbours of the Soviet Union in a way in which the Americans are not. Neighbours do not always get on well with one another and this has been particularly true of neighbouring states, but the fact of being neighbours also contains the promise of co-operation, especially when there is a common interest at stake. West Europeans, Japanese and Russians have two important common interests: one is in developing economic relationships, and the other is in avoiding war.

Paradoxically, one way of avoiding war is to make sure that the Americans retain some presence in the two regions, an interest which the Russians share but which they would never admit. Another is to reassure the Russians of one's peaceful intentions through fostering trade and other relationships. A third is to co-operate with all those countries in the so-called Third World which are alarmed by the tendency of the superpowers to extend their rivalry into other regions.

Such countries may be tempted to exploit the rivalry, but this is a dangerous game. Any switch from dependence on one superpower to dependence on the other may encourage the rejected power to support subversive elements within the country or to arm hostile neighbours. The resentment of superpower imperialism may be real enough, though difficult to translate into action. Europeans and Japanese, therefore, have opportunities to foster relationships which are not to be interpreted as attempts to impose a third imperialism, but offer a more disinterested support to the developing countries. Cultivation of the Third World could be an important means of preventing a further escalation of superpower rivalries which threaten to engulf the whole world.

Security in a Changing International Environment

The various policy objectives sketched above are often discussed in isolation within Western Europe or Japan. It is easier to see how they might be furthered by the West European states or by Japan, but much more difficult to conceive as forming the basis of a coordinated approach between them. However, coordination would be not only more effective, but would also establish a powerful new influence in world politics.

The Link between Europe and Japan

The background and differences in the situation of the West European states and Japan are so great that any attempt to link their security problems appears to be rather far-fetched and speculative. Moreover, their mutual relationship has been anything but harmonious, and since the 1970s bedevilled by economic friction. Because of their history as late modernizers in reaction to the threat from the superior technological civilization of the West, the Japanese have always been aware of Europe and assiduous students of its culture and institutions. The Europeans, on the whole, have paid fleeting attention to Japan, and then only as part of the exotic and mysterious orient. Later, this attitude was to be mingled with feelings of disgust and hatred in some of the countries affected by Japan's military expansion during the Second World War.

After the war Japan effectively disappeared from the European horizon, thought of first as an American protectorate and then as a people doing remarkable things with their economy. That was fine as long as the Japanese economy made little impact on Europe. However, in the 1970s Japanese exports to the members of EEC increased at a startling rate, while European exports to Japan increased only very slowly. Economic friction between Japan and the United States at the end of the 1960s was largely responsible for the accelerating Japanese drive into the European market, with the consequences which are very much with us today.[23]

The extremely unbalanced trade structure between Europe and Japan has been the principal area of contention, but competition in third markets and for resources has added to the friction. The Europeans, for example, have been anxious over the prospect of Japanese domination of the Chinese market, as revealed in the concern over the terms on which Japan was prepared to provide loans to China.[24] Economic friction is likely to continue in the 1980s, but a new element of co-operation and interlacing between the European and Japanese economies will probably also make itself felt, particularly through Japanese investments in Europe.

The difficult economic relationship and especially the Japanese threat to some European industries have provoked all the old European reflexes from the interwar peiod. When the argument about unfair competition through sweated and cheap labour could no longer be sustained, the Japanese were accused of unfair trading practices, of being cunning, and of hidden protectionism. The bad feeling is reflected in the headlines of the press. Here is a random sample taken from the period between 28 January and 14 February 1978: 'Japanese fail to satisfy EEC'; 'EEC reported irate over Japanese Surplus'; 'UK Warning to Japan over Protectionism'; 'Chill at Tokyo-EEC Talks'.[25]

This is hardly a good basis on which to build friendly international relations, let alone political co-operation. On the contrary, one might ask whether the conflict in the economic sphere is not going to spill over in some form or another into political conflict as has so often been the case in the past. Japan has the added disadvantage of having a generally bad cultural image among many Europeans, notably in Britain and perhaps least in Germany. The image is compounded by ignorance, memories of the Pacific War, and a lingering sense of European superiority. All three are fortunately on the decline, and can be expected to disappear with the rise of a generation whose minds are uncluttered by the stereotypes of the past.

In spite of the economic and cultural obstacles in the way of collaboration, it is striking that at the political level the contacts and consultations have multiplied steadily. To date they have been primarily confined to bilateral meetings of the foreign and economic affairs ministers of the major European states and Japan, interspersed with occasional state visits. Such encounters have usually ended with platitudinous statements designed to avoid any commitments and not to offend anyone. Nevertheless, these têtes-à-têtes have been conducted against the background of important changes in the international scene, and the practice of mutual consultation has laid the foundation for what might become one day a more serious and purposeful collaboration.

The changes in the international environment include Japan's phenomenal rise to the position of an economic power of global importance. The Europeans can no longer dismiss it as a troublesome entrepreneur who does not know or chooses to ignore the rules. Japan has to be accepted as an equal partner in the management of the world's economy. The Japanese, for their part, have come to appreciate that economic strength brings with it political influence and responsibilities. Individually, the European states, with the exception of Germany, cannot measure up to Japan's position in the world, but combined in the Common Market they dispose of greater economic power than Japan. They are aware that political influence and responsibility, which they have long been accustomed to exercise as individual nation states, are best pursued in common rather than from a weaker national base.

The rise of Europe and Japan has also corresponded to a relative decline of the United States, although it is still the most important economy in the world. The erosion of American military predominance in the face of the expansion and sophistication of Soviet nuclear armament and the global reach of Soviet power has also contributed to the greater political prominence of Western Europe and Japan, which see themselves more as equals than as subordinates in their association with the United States.

Just as Europeans and Japanese have only begun to think about the implications of their changed circumstances, so the superpowers have yet to adjust to the changes in their bilateral relationship and in the world at large. It is easier to see the problem that confronts the United States: it is primarily a matter of coming to grips with the reality of the global reach of Soviet military power and the unwillingness of the allies to accept American leadership unquestioningly, coupled with the fact of America's own increasing dependence on allied support. The Russians, given their record, are likely to find the learning process more difficult. They may want détente and arms control for the sake of their own economy, but they are apparently unable to change the structure of their empire in Eastern Europe sufficiently so that a relaxed relationship with the West does not immediately threaten to destabilize its social and political system.

The changing international environment is promoting a shared perception of security interests in Europe and Japan, despite differences in the regional background and difficulties in coordinating policies. Both Europe and Japan need security against political and military pressure from the Soviet Union, and this continues to be the principal function of their relations with the United States. But the United States is no longer able or willing to assume the main burden of Western defence as it has done in the past. Similarly, the Western allies can no longer afford to let the United States act as their sole spokesman in relations with the Soviet Union. The issue of access to the world's markets, its sources of energy, food and industrial raw materials has created a further commonality of interest — and a potential source of friction — between Western Europe and Japan, which in turn has a bearing on their relations with the superpowers.

The events of the Iranian revolution and the Soviet invasion of Afghanistan in 1979 and 1980 are graphic illustrations of the problems thrown up by these changing relationships. Over Iran Japan behaved as if it were an associate of the EEC. It was the first time that consultations between the European Community and Japan transcended bilateral or trilateral economic problems, and involved a search for a common policy in a complex international crisis. This novel development had several aspects. First, Japan, true to style, wanted to see what the members of the Community were going to do before making its own decisions. Secondly, the Europeans and Japanese came together as friends of the United States, but acutely aware that their material interests might be threatened by American actions. Thirdly, they were agreed that, from their point of view, to attempt a military solution to the crisis would probably be disastrous.

Over Afghanistan the Japanese and Europeans felt that they had been insufficiently consulted by the Americans. But whereas the Europeans paid lip-service to economic sanctions and continued to do business with the Soviet Union, the Japanese felt aggrieved because they had applied the sanctions loyally if reluctantly. This experience was the reason for their insistence on prior consultations over any coordinated Western response in the event of a Russian invasion of Poland.[26]

Britain, France, the Federal Republic of Germany and Japan, great powers in modern times, are still great powers today in so far as they have general interests as distinct from the limited interests of lesser powers. But these interests are not commensurate with their military strength. Nor do they have some of the other traditional attributes which went with great-power status in the past. They are outclassed by the superpowers, which are the only real global military powers today, and by some of the great regional states which have the potential to rival the superpowers in geographical extent, population and natural resources.

The peculiarity of the subjects of this study lies in their economic and technological importance and the intangible qualities of their societies, which include the tradition of thinking and acting like great powers. Of the four, Britain and France have been particularly well endowed with the latter, while Germany and Japan are endowed with the former. All thus share a sense of global importance.

In an international system dominated by the superpowers, whose relationship is moving into a transitory state with a greater Soviet ability to project power far from the homeland, thereby increasing Western feelings of insecurity, the four states might well turn to the traditional method of ensuring their security and of asserting their status and influence by acquiring greater military strength. This has been the rationale behind the British and French nuclear forces, and today influential voices in Japan are urging substantial rearmament. But the outstanding postwar success of West Germany and Japan has been achieved in spite of and perhaps because of the limitations on their military strength. This study, therefore, is concerned with new directions in the policies of the four states and with the place of the military dimension in such policies.

Notes

1. The definition that great powers are powers with 'general interests' emerged at the Paris Peace Conference of 1919. Martin Wight, *Power Politics* (edited by Hedley Bull and Carsten Holbraad, Harmondsworth, Penguin Books for the Royal Institute of International Affairs, 1979), p. 50.

2. Ibid., p. 53. Bertrand Russell describes the drive to domination rather starkly:

Every State which is sufficiently powerful aims at foreign conquest; apparent instances to the contrary only arise where a State, from experience, knows itself to be less strong than it seems, or, from inexperience, believes itself to be less strong than it is. The broad rule is that a State conquers what it can, and stops only when it reaches a frontier at which some other State or States can exert a pressure as strong as its own.

Bertrand Russell, *Power: A New Social Analysis* (London, Allen & Unwin, 1938), pp. 166-7.

3. Such far-sightedness was found in particular among men of science. P.M.S. Blackett is perhaps the best known among them; Sir Henry Tizard was another. He was converted from a belief that Britain should have a 'balanced' defence, including atomic weapons and other strategic systems, to a conviction that it should not make atomic weapons at all. He wrote in 1949:

We persist in regarding ourselves as a Great Power, capable of everything and only temporarily handicapped by economic difficulties. We are not a Great Power and never will be again. We are a great nation, but if we begin to behave like a Great Power we shall soon cease to be a great nation. Let us take warning from the fate of the Great Powers of the past and not burst ourselves with pride (See Aesop's fable of the frog).

Quoted in Margaret Gowing, *Independence and Deterrence: Britain and Atomic*

Energy, 1945-1952, Vol. I Policy Making (London, Macmillan, 1974), p. 229.

4. The conservative coalition of the Christian Democratic Union and the Bavarian-based Christian Social Union. This last event has in fact happened with the resignation of Helmut Schmidt on 1 October 1982, and the installation of the leader of the CDU, Helmut Kohl, as Chancellor.

5. For a brief discussion of this point, see Wolf Mendl, 'Moral Principles and Power Politics – The People's Republic of China in the United Nations', in Nicholas Sims (ed.), *Explorations in Ethics and International Relations* (London, Croom Helm, 1981), pp. 21-44. Samuel S. Kim, *China, The United Nations, and World Order* (Princeton, NJ, Princeton Univ. Press, 1979) offers a very substantial analysis of China's role in the UN.

6. For a discussion of the Nigerian predicament, see F.O. Adisa, *The Development of Nigeria's Defence Policy: 1960-1979* (unpublished Ph.D thesis, University of London, 1983).

7. The impact of a conservative political philosophy on statesmanship is discussed by Anibal Romero in *The Conservative Challenge: Kissinger and the Ideological Crisis of American Foreign Policy* (unpublished Ph.D thesis, University of London, 1984).

8. For this view, see Hedley Bull, *The Anarchical Society: A Study of Order in International Politics* (London, Macmillan, 1977), p. 203. For a discussion of the classification of powers, see Wight, Chapters I-5, pp. 23-67.

9. Bull, pp. 101-2.

10. This is in contrast to a definition which describes the balance of power as 'an equilibrium or a roughly equal distribution of power between two opponents, the opposite, then, of hegemony or domination.' Arnold Wolfers, *Discord and Collaboration: Essays on International Politics* (Baltimore, The Johns Hopkins Press, 1968), p. 118.

11. Its origin is attributed to Vegetius (383-450 AD), 'Qui desiderat pacem, praeparet bellum', *Epitome Institutorum Rei Militaris*, 3rd prolog. See Georg Büchmann, *Geflügelte Worte* (Berlin, Verlag der Haude & Spenerschen Buchhandlung, 1905), p. 511.

12. Dennis Ross, *Incremental or Comprehensive SALT: Is some SALT better than no SALT?* (Los Angeles, Center for International and Strategic Affairs, University of California, May 1979), pp. 12-14. See also John Erickson, 'The Soviet View of Deterrence: A General Survey' (*Survival*, vol. XXIV no. 6, November/December 1982), pp. 242-51.

13. To be distinguished from the *control* of crises. See Bull, p. 208.

14. 'together and with God's help we can and will resolve the problems which confront us. Why shouldn't we believe that? After all, we are Americans.' *Guardian*, 21 January 1981.

15. *Basic Principles of Relations between the United States of America and the Union of Soviet Socialist Republics*, 29 May 1972.

The following extracts illustrate the point I am trying to make:

> Second: the U.S.A. and the U.S.S.R. attach major importance to preventing the development of situations capable of causing a dangerous exacerbation of their relations. Therefore, they will do their utmost to avoid military confrontation and to prevent the outbreak of nuclear war. They will always exercise restraint in their mutual relations, and will be prepared to negotiate and settle dfferences by peaceful means. Discussions and negotiations on outstanding issues will be conducted in a spirit of reciprocity, mutual accommodation and mutual benefit.
>
> Both sides recognize that efforts to obtain unilateral advantage at the expense of the other, directly or indirectly, are inconsistent with these objectives. The prerequisites for maintaining and strengthening peaceful

Security in a Changing International Environment

relations between the U.S.A. and the U.S.S.R. are the recognition of the security interests of the parties ...
Third: The U.S.A. and the U.S.S.R. have a special responsibility, as do other countries which are members of the United Nations Security Council, to do everything in their power so that conflicts or situations will not arise which would serve to increase international tensions.
Fourth: The U.S.A. and the U.S.S.R. intend to widen the juridical basis of their mutual relations and to exert the necessary efforts so that bilateral agreements which they have concluded and multilateral treaties and agreements to which they are jointly parties are faithfully implemented.
Tenth: The U.S.A. and the U.S.S.R. will seek to ensure that their ties and cooperation in all the above-mentioned fields and in any others in their mutual interest are built on a firm and long-term basis ...

The two partners felt constrained to add a paragraph designed to reassure the rest of the world:

Eleventh: the U.S.A. and the U.S.S.R. make no claim for themselves and would not recognize the claims of anyone else to any special rights or advantages in world affairs. They recognize the sovereign equality of all states.
The development of U.S.-Soviet relations is not directed against third countries and their interests.

London, *United States Information Service*, American Embassy, 30 May 1972.
16. A. Ross Johnson, *The Warsaw Pact: Soviet Military Policy in Eastern Europe* (Rand Paper 6583, Santa Monica, Cal., The Rand Corporation, July 1981), p. 36.
17. Herman Kahn, *On Thermonuclear War* (Princeton, NJ, Princeton Unversity Press, 1960); *Thinking About the Unthinkable* (London, Weidenfeld, 1962); *On Escalation: Metaphors and Scenarios* (London, Pall Mall Press, 1965).
18. The evolution of nuclear war-fighting doctrines in the United States is briefly and critically examined by Phil Williams in 'Deterrence, Warfighting and American Strategy', *ADIU Report* (Armament and Disarmament Information Unit, Sussex University), vol. V, no. 1, January/February 1983, pp. 1-5.
19. For a discussion of this problem, see Christoph Bertram, 'Rethinking Arms Control', *Foreign Affairs*, vol. LIX, no. 2, Winter 1980/81, pp. 352-65.
20. For a discussion of this concept see Wight, Chapter 16, pp. 168-85.
21. The best published sources of information about the current state of the Soviet armed forces and defence are the publications of the US Arms Control and Disarmament Agency; the annual *Military Balance* published by the International Institute for Strategic Studies (London); and the *Yearbook of World Armaments and Disarmament* published by the Stockholm International Peace Research Institute (SIPRI).
22. Carefully reasoned analyses of Soviet military policy, which try to be as objective as possible, may be found in the annual *Strategic Survey* of the International Institute for Strategic Studies and the more recent annual *Asian Security* of the Research Institute for Peace and Security, Tokyo, first published in 1979.
23. Klaus Terfloth, 'Brussels and Tokyo: Dialogue between Economic Giants', in Curt Gasteyger (ed.), *Japan and the Atlantic World* (Peterborough, Hants, Saxon House for the Atlantic Institute for International Affairs, November 1972), pp. 73-4.
24. *Japan Times Weekly*, 9 September 1978; David Morris, 'The Strengthening Japan-China Links' (*Japan*, London, Anglo-Japanese Economic Institute,

November 1978, pp. 7-11); *Guardian*, 2 July 1979.

25. *Guardian*, 30 January 1978; *International Herald Tribune*, 28/29 January 1978; *Financial Times*, 28 January 1978; *Daily Telegraph*, 14 February 1978.

26. *Japan Times Weekly*, 20 December 1980; *Japan* (London, Japan Information Centre, Embassy of Japan), no. 139, 25 March 1981.

2 THE MILITARY DIMENSION

In today's world a country's power and influence are basically determined by its economic performance.[1]

Few would want to quarrel with this statement, nor with the order of priorities of foreign policy listed in the same report from which the quotation is taken:

1. National Security
2. Economic and Social Well-being
3. Honouring Commitments (such as the terms of alliances, the protection of dependent territories and of individual citizens)
4. A Peaceful and Just World[2]

The four states which form the subject of this study would surely subscribe to these objectives, though they might phrase them somewhat differently. One can imagine the French replacing 'National Security' with 'National Independence' or 'Honouring Commitments' with 'Defence of French Interests', or the Japanese giving a 'Peaceful World' a higher rating and a category of its own.

If the quotation at the head of this chapter is accepted as laying down the correct criterion for 'power' and 'influence', then Japan and Germany must be included in the first rank of nations, with France somewhere on the borderline between the first and second ranks, and Britain trailing some way behind France, well in the second rank. Be that as it may, there can be no doubt that the governments of all four states would regard the assurance of national security as their central concern.

Looking back over the history of the past thirty-five years, we find the actual use of military power has at the most played a subordinate role in ensuring their security and protecting their interests. Only France has been involved in a protracted and major military effort in defence of national interests; first in Indochina (where only professional soldiers, drawn mainly from the colonial army, were used) and then in Algeria. Those were hardly good examples of the effectiveness of military force, although one could argue that on a strictly military level the army had been successful in Algeria. Britain's military operations in the postwar era were reminiscent of the imperial policing of earlier days and can be seen in retrospect as a series of rearguard actions. Germany and Japan have not even used their military forces in minor actions.

This modest record of military activity would suggest that military power has been of secondary importance in securing the national interest. Indeed, Japanese and German power and influence in the world today seem to be in inverse proportion to their military strength. On the other hand, official rhetoric, echoed by popular belief, and the financial and industrial effort put into armaments by some of the governments, point to the opposite conclusion. Blindness to the evidence of the postwar experience is, however, not the only, or even the most important explanation for this contradiction. We must turn to more subtle psychological reasons and the changed function of military power for a clearer understanding of this paradox.

The overriding problem of the security of Western Europe and Japan since the Second World War has been the presence on their doorsteps of a militarily superior Soviet Union, espousing an antagonistic social and political system under cover of which it has greatly expanded its empire since the Second World War. Relations with Russia are discussed in detail in Chapter 4. Suffice it to note here that they have passed through various phases and have not been uniformly hostile. In the immediate aftermath of the war the Soviet 'threat' appeared to be more political than military, with Russian support for strong communist parties and left-wing movements that flourished in the chaos of ruined and impoverished societies. The Berlin Blockade of 1948-9 and the outbreak of the Korean War ushered in a period of extreme hostility in which the armed strength of communism became the most important threat.

By the mid-1950s the danger of Soviet military aggression seemed to have receded and was replaced by a greater equilibrium between East and West, which reflected the military balance between the two superpowers. In Europe, danger was not seen as coming primarily from the threat of a Soviet attack, but from uprisings in East Europe which might provoke a general crisis and lead to unpredictable Russian behaviour.

The rapid expansion of Soviet military power in the 1970s revived the more traditional perception of military strength as the instrument of aggressive designs. Europeans and Japanese are, however, convinced that in the final analysis military security against the Soviet Union can be provided only by the United States. This proposition might have been true if nuclear weapons had never been invented, but the nuclear dimension and the special relationship it has led to between the superpowers, as described in Chapter 1, has introduced a novel element into the security problems of the four states.

As a consequence, the role of defence in their national policies has assumed a rather different aspect from that of before the war. This does not mean that all have seen it in the same light. On the contrary, they have approached it from opposite directions. Britain and France have placed primary emphasis on their military capabilities because initially they wanted to return to their prewar status among the powers; hence the impulse to acquire their own nuclear armament. On the other hand, since their independence the Federal Republic of Germany and Japan have placed a much lower emphasis on military power in their efforts to break with their militaristic past, and once again have become fully accepted members of the international community. In this chapter special attention will be devoted to the military policies of the four states, and for this reason it is easiest to discuss them in pairs.

Britain and France

Their objective was to return to 'normal', which meant seeing and conducting themselves as the great powers they had always been, in a world altered by the war but operating on the lines it has always done. While the perceptions of their place in the world may have been similar, if not identical, their policies had very different orientations.

Britain was intent on continuing with its 'imperial' mission, though under the postwar Labour Government this was understood as an orderly progress towards self-government and eventual statehood in the dependent territories. The extent of the British Empire made it inevitable that Britain regarded itself as having worldwide responsibilities. The transformation of Empire into Commonwealth made little difference and the imperial assumptions remained. The independence of the states in the Indian subcontinent had no serious impact on strategic thinking. For many years afterwards Britain retained a network of bases around the Indian Ocean at enormous cost and effort, though the heart of the empire had long since been taken out.[3]

The British recognized that the United States and the Soviet Union had achieved new heights of power which Britain, even with its Empire/ Commonwealth, could not hope to reach, but they considered themselves to be in a special category of world power behind the two giants.[4] The policy towards Europe resumed where it had left off at the outbreak of war. From the earliest years of this century it had been a fundamental British objective to involve the United States in the European balance of power, an objective which was realised in both World Wars. However, after 1945 there appeared two qualitative changes in Britain's policy. The first came immediately after the war with the recognition of a basic dependence on American protection against a potential Soviet threat, or for that matter any kind of hegemonial threat on the continent of Europe. The second came in 1954 with the indefinite commitment of British troops to the defence of the West on the European mainland.

These changes implied a loss of flexibility in British policy, though it is doubtful whether this was fully recognized at the time. Britain had become dependent on the United States in the economic and military spheres and had lost some of its freedom of manoeuvre. This reality was partly disguised under what was called 'the Special Relationship', which, however, could not hide the fact that the United States was the senior partner. Thus, it was believed that participation in the Korean War was the price that had to be paid for an American commitment to Europe. In the 1960s Britain was the only West European ally to give strong diplomatic support to the United States over the war in Vietnam. Britain has been the most enthusiastic supporter of American policies for the Atlantic Alliance — though not necessarily the most ardent in carrying them out. The United States has also played an important role in British defence policy formulation, whether it was through an agreement to buy British equipment in return for the decision to buy the F-111 aircraft, or through the exercise of pressure to delay the announcement of a firm date for the withdrawal from east of Suez.[5]

If Britain continued its basic prewar policy towards the United States in a modified form, the same can also be said of policy towards the Soviet Union. Russia was seen as a potential enemy in Europe and elsewhere. The need to protect an Indian empire had gone, but there were other reasons why the British thought it necessary to have a military presence in the Middle East and South-east Asia. The oil of the Middle East and the raw materials of Malaya had to be 'protected'; communist subversion had to be eliminated; lines of communication through the Suez Canal and across the Indian Ocean to East Asia and the Antipodes had to be maintained, and so on.[6]

France faced a different agenda for its return to great-power status. Economic and social reconstruction was essential before the French could reassert their independence, resume their leadership in Europe, and recover their empire. As it turned out, they set about these tasks simultaneously, with mixed success. Beneath the political chaos of the Fourth Republic a remarkably efficient and purposeful administrative elite laid the foundations for the recovery and renovation of French society. After an initial attempt to play a traditional role in European politics, which meant collaborating with the Soviet Union over the issue of Germany, the oncoming Cold War led to a new approach: reconciliation with West Germany through the construction of the European communities under Franco-German leadership, but with France as the senior partner. The recovery of empire turned out to be a mirage and was an unmitigated disaster, wasting precious resources and national energies. Some, however, might argue that it was a blessing in disguise since it led directly to the return of de Gaulle in 1958.

In the early postwar years France, alongside the other states of Western Europe, relied heavily on American assistance for economic recovery. The assistance was twofold: an active participation in economic reconstruction through the Marshall Plan and other measures, and the provision of a shield against the Red Army; not that anyone seriously believed that the Russians would attack, except for a brief spell of anxiety immediately after the outbreak of the Korean War. When the Americans put great pressure on the Europeans to rearm, the Europeans feared that it might undermine the process of recovery. This was especially so in countries with large communist parties, where it was argued that concentration on defence at the expense of economic welfare was the surest way in which to undermine their security.

France rearmed reluctantly, and soon diverted most of its military effort overseas. Once the nuclear programme got under way, especially after the return of de Gaulle, the military effort received a new sense of direction. However, French policy was firmly Europe-centered, even at the height of the colonial wars. France used its nuclear arms to justify a posture as a world power, but it did not distribute its military forces in penny packets around the world once it was rid of the war in Algeria. Instead, they were deployed in Europe and a few key areas in Africa.

There was no scope for returning to the old game of power politics in Europe in the shadow of Soviet-American domination, and so policy concentrated on establishing a position of leadership in Western Europe. That has been the real centre of French attention both before and after de Gaulle. Within this narrow field France has tried to assert its 'seniority' over the Federal Republic of Germany; has, through the Franco-German partnership, prevented Britain from its traditional game of playing off the West European states against each other; and has done everything possible to challenge American domination of the Western Alliance, while accepting the need for an American presence on the front line against the Eastern bloc.[7]

The French view of the Soviet Union also differs from that of Britain. For the French, the Russians have been both partners and opponents in the management of Europe. The brief period of collaboration after the war was partially revived in de Gaulle's vision of a Europe from the Atlantic to the Urals, and was noticed again in 1980 in the rivalry with the Federal Republic over who was to be Russia's privileged interlocutor. On the other hand, there has always been a strong undercurrent of fear of communism in French society, which has ebbed and flowed with the tides of domestic affairs. The French Communist Party (PCF) has a tradition of loyalty to the Soviet Union, although there have been periods of estrangement. Many Frenchmen, therefore, are haunted by the spectre of a Trojan Horse in their midst.

The presence of communist ministers in the socialist government of M. Mauroy has not so far (the spring of 1983) appeared to have had a noticeable effect on foreign policy. On the contrary, France under President Mitterand seems set to pursue a tougher line towards the Soviet Union than did the France of President Giscard d'Estaing. Indeed, French policy towards the Atlantic Alliance is more positive now than it has ever been since the beginning of the Fifth Republic. That is not to say that the French communists have become 'Atlanticists'. Communist ministers hold no portfolios directy concerned with foreign affairs and defence and, more important, the apparent quiescence of the party reflects its weak electoral position and the dictates of political strategy. When they judge the time to be ripe, the communists will not hesitate to break with their socialist partners, but it is more likely that they will do so over domestic rather than external policies, for it is on economic and social issues that they have the best hope of regaining popular support.

Generally speaking, therefore, the imperial legacy, perceptions of the national 'role', broad objectives of foreign policy, and the security relationship with the United States have shaped the place that Britain and France have accorded to nuclear weapons and conventional forces in their national security policies.

The first Russian atomic explosion in 1949 profoundly modified the objectives of the British nuclear programme. Until then the United Kingdom sought information and some special materials from the United States to assist it in developing the production of fissile material and weapons independently. The Soviet explosion brought home to the British that they were outclassed by the United States and the Soviet Union. Although the goal of acquiring a national atomic industry was not abandoned, the British were prepared to give up their autonomy in weapons production, provided they could have a stock of bombs under their own control. In the long drawn-out and complicated negotiations which followed the new orientation in British policy, the Americans consistently opposed this form of 'integration', and demanded nothing less than the abandonment of the British atomic enterprise.[8]

Under no circumstances would the British accept such terms, and henceforth they embarked on the uneasy course between dependence on the United States and the assertion of national independence in the nuclear sphere which distinguishes their policy today. When the time was ripe for a decision on whether to proceed from the production of nuclear to the production of thermonuclear weapons, the government opted for the H-bomb, arguing that it would contribute to the general deterrent posture of the West, that it would be an instrument of passive deterrence against Soviet blackmail, and that it would help to preserve British influence in diplomacy towards the superpowers and arms control/disarmament negotiations. The Labour leadership, though not all the rank and file, supported the H-bomb decision, but rejected the strategic argument that it was a more reliable substitute for the American deterrent. This distinction forced the government to justify its policy on the grounds of great power status, as summarized by Prime Minister Macmillan in an interview on television:

> The independent contribution gives us a better position in the world, it gives us a better position with respect to the United States. It puts us where we ought to be, in the position of a great power. The fact that we have it makes the United States pay a greater regard to our point of view, and that is of great importance.[9]

This line of argument held sway for a long time, but has gradually lapsed as the alleged British influence over American policy began to lose its credibility. Today we are back at the argument that an independent deterrent is essential for our security against the Soviet Union. One can think of a number of explanations for the retention of a nuclear capability, such as the inadvisability of leaving France as the sole nuclear-weapons state in Western Europe or the sheer problem of dismantling and abandoning nuclear forces, but the suggestion that it is essential for protection against the Soviet Union is hardly credible.

Is it conceivable that the Soviet Union would threaten Britain with nuclear weapons outside the context of a major international crisis involving the United States? In such an event Britain's very limited nuclear capability is unlikely to have much impact on the course of events. The decisions will be made in Moscow and Washington on their mutual assessment of the superpower balance. Even in the improbable event of a direct Anglo-Soviet confrontation without American involvement, is it credible that a prime minister even as tough as Mrs Thatcher would issue an order for the wholesale destruction of Britain? Moreover, the experience of the past thirty-odd years suggests that this is not the way in which the Soviet Union would operate. Russian policy is governed by assessments of the degree of 'ripeness' of a society for intervention, and is marked by a determination to avoid unnecessary risks. As long as Britain is allied to the United States, a direct confrontation with Britain would be a very risky undertaking.

Another and less speculative set of reasons for questioning the official British position relates to doubts about the 'independence' of the British deterrent. There are, of course, clauses in the various nuclear agreements between Britain and the United States which allow for independent use in an extreme emergency,[10] but it is inconceivable that such use could be made of the deterrent without American approval and assistance. Britain's dependence on the United States in nuclear matters was confirmed in two mutual defence agreements signed in August 1958 and May 1959. They provided for a full exchange of information on weapon designs and effects and of nuclear intelligence data; for the abandonment of Britain's independent testing programme; and for a division of labour in which the production of the enriched uranium U235 was to be concentrated in the United States and the production of plutonium in Britain, the materials to be exchanged at a fixed rate of one gramme of plutonium for 1.76 grammes of U235. The agreements were renewed in 1969 and 1979.[11]

The effect of these agreements has meant that, apart from the missiles for nuclear submarines bought under the Nassau Agreement of 1962 and the agreement in 1980 to purchase the Trident, the fuel for British submarine reactors plus some of the material for the missile warheads originates in the United States. This, added to joint targeting arrangements, the use of common communication facilities, and the many other shared security arrangements from the stationing of American military aircraft in Britain to the use of Holy Loch by the US Navy, means that in terms of technology and deployment the British nuclear force cannot be regarded as fully independent. It may fulfil

The Military Dimension

a variety of diplomatic and political functions, but it is not a really autonomous instrument of defence.

The opposite is true of the French nuclear deterrent. France established its *Commissariat à l'Energie Atomique* amid the ruins and chaos of the aftermath of war. From the start it was clear that the development of nuclear weapons, official declarations to the contrary notwithstanding, was considered to be a potential function of the nuclear programme. Although French scientists had collaborated in the allied nuclear programme during the war and had provided the British with valuable knowledge, skills and material, they had no official status. The British were prepared to go some way to recognizing the French claim to be regarded as partners in the allied effort, but this was not accepted by the Americans.

When the United States cut off the British from nuclear collaboration both during and after the war, the British worked ceaselessly to restore the old relationship and were justified in expecting some measure of success, though at a price. France tried the same approach, hoping through its own efforts and achievements to persuade the Americans to relax the restrictions on co-operation, but to no avail.[12] Attempts at collaboration with Britain met a similar fate, largely because of Britain's entanglement with the United States in these matters.[13] So, in effect, the French had to go it alone, though not entirely because French technicians had benefited from American papers contributed to international conferences on atomic energy and from personal contacts with their American colleagues.

Great play has been made of the contrast between British dependence and French independence in the nuclear field. In fact, however, the evidence points to a persistent French desire to establish a collaborative relationship with the 'Anglo-Saxon' powers, and this desire continued well into the Gaullist period. In the end it was the combination of American intransigence and de Gaulle's concept of the destiny of France that laid the foundation of an independent French nuclear strategy. Here, too, there were some similarities and some contrasts with the British experience.

In both countries there was a dearth of strategic thought and analysis about the function of nuclear weapons before they came on-stream. The public arguments for having nuclear weapons at all were conducted almost exclusively in a diplomatic and political context. This applied both to the proponents and opponents of a national nuclear armament. It is still very largely true in Britain today. The French, on the other hand, were forced by circumstances to develop a military rationale for their national nuclear force. The first important attempt to do so was published in the year of the first nuclear test explosion,[14] and there has been a substantial literature on the subject since then.

The evolution of French strategic doctrine has followed closely on the development of French nuclear capabilities. Until the arrival on the scene of tactical nuclear weapons, the doctrine was firmly anchored in the theory of minimal and proportionate deterrence and, apart from some vague hints about a 'European' bomb, there was little pretence that the deterrent served anything except the interests of France. With the decline of classic Gaullism and the greater sophistication of French weaponry in the mid-1970s, there came a shift in emphasis towards graduated response and a forward strategy. Since this only made sense if it included French deployments in Germany, emphasis was laid on the need to coordinate defence with the allies. At the beginning of the 1980s France is uneasily poised between a continued assertion of the absolute independence of the national deterrent and the realities of its strategic situation which requires a measure of co-operation with its allies.

The other basic objective in its nuclear policy: the re-establishment of its position as a leader in Europe — a claim founded on the Franco-German partnership — has also had unexpected consequences. The Federal Republic of Germany has become Europe's most important economic power and America's most important ally in Europe because of its strategic position on the continent. The Federal Republic's policy very largely determines whether the Americans will continue to guarantee the security of Western Europe with their physical presence. If by chance that presence were to be removed, then it will be the West Germans who will decide Europe's future. They could decide to throw their weight behind the establishment of an alternative West European security system, of which the French deterrent and what remains of a *British* deterrent, if the break with the United States also applied to Britain, would be key components, or they might be attracted to a settlement with the Soviet Union and sign a new 'Treaty of Rapallo' — a recurrent nightmare among the French.[15] Thus, in terms of diplomatic weight, it is Germany which is the 'senior' partner, for it holds the key to the security of Europe.

In regard to military policy, combining the nuclear and conventional elements, the experience of Britain and France has revealed a disproportion between means and ends, for which the military are not necessarily to blame. For instance, a British Staff paper concluded in

The Military Dimension

the summer of 1956 that the United Kingdom had borne too heavy a defence burden since 1945 and that this had contributed to the recurrent economic crises. It urged that a priority should be given to stabilising the economy.[16] Such a far-sighted and disinterested approach was reinforced by the requirements of long-term planning. When it takes five years to design, develop and produce a warship with twenty years' life in service, and ten years to do the same for an aircraft with a life-span of ten years, it is imperative to form some sort of picture of the likely technological, strategic and international environment in ten years' time. This sense of urgency is absent in the Foreign Office, where the Policy Planning Department has a lowly status, and where there is a tradition of tackling issues as they arise.[17]

There are a number of examples where military policy has not matched national resources, or where policy has been conducted on traditional but mistaken assumptions about the usefulness of military means to further the national interest. An example of the first is Britain's failure in the early postwar years to make clear choices between nuclear deterrence and the requirements of widespread overseas commitments. The result was a compromise between deterrence and defence strategies which left both short of adequate resources.[18] An example of the second was the balance sheet at the end of the ill-fated Anglo-French expedition of November 1956 to occupy the Suez Canal. On the military side there were 22 dead, 96 wounded and the loss of 8 aircraft. On the economic side the expedition had cost £35 million, gold and dollar reserves fell by £100 million, and more than £2,000 million were required before the balance of payments crisis could be brought under control. To top it all, there was a 50 per cent increase in the cost of shipping oil via the Cape route as a consequence of Nasser's response to the attack by blocking the Suez Canal.[19]

The failures of British policy can be attributed directly to a lack of understanding of the changed security environment of the postwar era and to a failure in imagination. British perceptions were clouded by 'great-power' thinking, and an inability to conceive of the possibility that the military instrument might no longer be appropriate in the pursuit of some national objectives. The French learnt the same lesson the hard way. From 1946 to 1962 they were engaged in almost continuous and futile colonial warfare. This in itself prevented any coherent approach to military policy.

It can be argued that since the end of the Algerian War French security policy has been based on a broad and comprehensive conceptual framework. On paper, at least, the triad of deterrent, conventional and territorial forces presents a unified whole, each with its mission complementary to the others. In practice, however, there are contradictions. Some are old, such as the budgetary ones: the conflict between the demands of nuclear and conventional forces, between equipment and personnel costs. Others are new, such as the contradiction between a policy that uses French paratroops to protect French interests in Africa, and the policy that accepts the need to foster the independence of African states. But the biggest paradox of all is the renewal of pressures for alliance integration brought about by a quite successful programme of creating a full range of 'independent' nuclear forces, which require a more sophisticated strategic doctrine of graduated response than the simpler Gaullist doctrine of minimal deterrence confined exclusively to the national territory.

West Germany and Japan

In 1945 Germany and Japan were defeated, occupied and demilitarized. Neither was to be allowed to have an autonomous security policy backed by a military establishment. The allies were determined to avoid the experience of the Versailles settlement after the First World War, which had left the core of the German army intact. But there were important differences in the situation of the two countries.

The German state was destroyed completely, and its eventual re-establishment was postulated on agreement among the allies. The policy of unconditional surrender had implied the transfer of authority over the state to the victorious powers. Therefore, the future of Germany could be decided only by agreement among the allies, and they were aware that such an agreement was essential if they wanted to avoid conflict among themselves.

At the Tehran Conference in December 1943 the United States, Russia and Britain agreed to divide Germany into four zones of occupation (France was to be invited to join them as an occupying power). The difficulties and dangers of such a course were obvious, but they still hoped to retain a unified approach to the German problem. Partition into four zones was seen as a preliminary to permanent dismemberment. A Control Commission was to be set up to coordinate allied policies and, most important as it turned out, they decided in September 1944 that Berlin should be jointly administered to symbolize their unified control.

At the Yalta and Potsdam Conferences in February and June/July 1945 the idea of dismemberment was more or less abandoned, and an indefinite partition into zones of occupation remained the only practicable policy since there was no thought of re-establishing central German administration.

Japan suffered a very different fate from that of Germany. The 'Proclamation to Japan' issued by the United States, the United Kingdom and Nationalist China, which was the basic allied document, was vague as to whether the Japanese government would be allowed to continue functioning and about the future status of the emperor.[20] The wording of the Instrument of Surrender, signed on board the USS *Missouri* in Tokyo Bay on 2 September 1945, seemed to confirm the continuity of the state.[21] Thus, its apparatus remained intact, and many of the officials who had administered the country before the war continued to do so now in spite of severe purges.

The occupation of Japan contrasted with that of Germany in two major aspects. It established a two-tier government of the country. General MacArthur, as Supreme Commander of the Allied Powers (SCAP), acted as effective ruler, though in theory under the control of the Far Eastern Commission of eleven allied states, which sat in Washington. Under him the Japanese government carried out his directives. In spite of the immense power and authority of SCAP, the Japanese were able to modify occupation policies in the light of what they perceived to be the national interest. After the change of direction in American policy from punishment and reform to rehabilitation and reconstruction, Japan became increasingly autonomous, except in the fields of security and external affairs.

The second characteristic was the extent of the *American* influence. The occupation was nominally in the name of the allied powers, and an Allied Council for Japan was set up in Tokyo. However, its functions were purely advisory and then only if asked. Moreover, the United States Government had the exclusive right to communicate with SCAP. Apart from a small zone of occupation reserved for the British Commonwealth in the west of the country, the allied personnel was exclusively American.[22]

The security problems of the two countries thus stem from their differing postwar environments. Germany was divided into four zones of occupation, in each of which the occupying power pursued its own policies. By 1948 the zones had been effectively reduced to two. The Allied Control Council maintained a semblance of four-power coordination, but it was little more than a fiction. On the other hand, the special status of Berlin ensured that Germany would, in fact, remain a four-power problem. Japan retained its unity under one occupying power which effectively controlled its postwar destiny.

Germany had no government. As a consequence, the break in continuity which led to the birth of the two German states, the issue of Berlin, and the residual rights of the four powers raised the problem of legitimacy which has still not been fully resolved. Continuity of the state was ensured in Japan, and the transition from occupation regime to full sovereignty was smooth.

Finally, Germany was and remains at the centre of the issue of European security. The same cannot be said of Japan's position in Asia. It became a keystone in the containment structure which the United States built in East Asia, but the core of the security problems of the region lay in the triangular relationship of the Soviet Union, the United States and China.

The consequences of their postwar fate are still relevant to the security policies of West Germany and Japan. The war has left a legacy of unfinished business to both. There is the issue of the legitimacy of the two German states; the problem of West Berlin; and the function of intra-German relationships as a barometer of East-West relations. Japan has an unresolved territorial claim against, and no formal peace treaty with the Soviet Union.

In spite of these problems both countries have been outstandingly successful in achieving unprecedented economic prosperity. This can be attributed in part to their complete demilitarization after the war. Subsequent rearmament has not been an economic burden for Japan. In the Federal Republic of Germany it has absorbed a greater share of the GNP, but the Germans had at least the first decade after the war when they were unencumbered by substantial military expenditures. The wholesale destruction of German and Japanese industry turned out to be a boon, enabling Germans and Japanese to install machinery and industrial organizations more attuned to the requirements of the second half of the century. The process was assisted further by the psychological shock of defeat and the destruction of old political and social values. France was also able to benefit in this way, whereas unoccupied and relatively undamaged Britain was lumbered with industrial plant and a traditional outlook among management and unions which were serious handicaps to its economic development.

Most important of all, however, the security of both countries has been embedded in remarkably durable alliance structures: the German Federal Republic in a multilateral and Japan in a bilateral system. These

The Military Dimension

alliances have not only coloured their security perspectives, but have to a large extent dictated the military dimension of their policies, which has several distinctive features.

The demilitarization of both countries immediately after the war was carried out with the overwhelming support of the people, weary of war and revolted by the excesses of militarism. It is now commonplace in Japan to insist that the postwar constitution with its war-renouncing Article IX was imposed by the American authorities. Although it is generally agreed that the article was originally drafted in the HQ of SCAP, it was not unwillingly accepted by the Japanese. The conservative leaders of the government may have had their reservations about its implications, but the people were content. For the West Germans there were no such constitutional prohibitions once the Federal Republic had come into being, but the demilitarization of West Germany had been just as popular as the demilitarization of Japan. Both countries accepted rearmament reluctantly as a price which had to be paid for the continued protection of the United States.

The new military establishments are subject to strict civilian control. In Japan they had to be disguised as 'Self-defence Forces' (SDF), and for a long time operated in the margins of legitimacy. The provisions of the constitution and the terms of the law under which the SDF were established ensure that the military play a subordinate part in the formulation of security policy. Despite mounting pressures for an increased role and a greater freedom of action for the armed forces, it is most unlikely that they will ever regain the dominant position in policy-making that they had acquired before the war. The military forces of the Federal Republic do not operate under the same constraints, and their constitutionality is not in doubt. Through the deliberate civilianizing of the soldier, the Germans have erected a different kind of barrier against the return of militarism. If we adopt Samuel Huntington's theoretical models of 'objective civilian control' and 'subjective civilian control',[23] then the management of Japan's defence approximates to the first and that of the Federal Republic to the second, but *both* confirm the supremacy of the civilians over the military, though reports of a planned military coup in Japan in June 1980 raise doubts whether some of the military have fully accepted this.

A second feature common to both is the strictly defensive orientation of their armed forces. In Japan this was the essential prerequisite for their establishment in the first place. A war of aggression is specifically prohibited by Article 26 of the Basic Law of the Federal Republic.[24] The difficulties of defining 'offensive' and 'defensive' weapons, and of deciding what is a war of aggression and what might be a 'defensive' pre-emptive attack may raise doubts about the practical application of such legal dispositions. Nevertheless, they have effectively prevented the German Federal Republic and Japan from conducting military operations outside the national territory. In theory, the Federal Republic has certain extra-territorial obligations under the terms of the Atlantic Alliance, and German troops have taken part in exercises outside the national territory. However, German forces are permanently stationed only in their country with responsibility for the Central Front which runs through Germany. Japan has no obligations to operate outside its territory under the terms of the treaty with the United States.

The third distinguishing feature is the inhibition over the development and possession of nuclear weapons. Strong popular dispositions in both countries against such weapons reinforce official policies. Japan's nuclear 'allergy' is natural enough, and since January 1968 every government has publicly adhered to the three non-nuclear principles: not to make, not to possess, not to introduce nuclear weapons into Japan. Germany is prohibited from making nuclear weapons under the terms of the London and Paris Agreements.[25] The non-nuclear status of the two countries, which have also signed and ratified the Non-Proliferation Treaty, is modified by the possession of nuclear technology and industries which could provide a base for the rapid development of nuclear armament.[26]

The Federal Republic of Germany and Japan, therefore, are new model 'powers'. They have returned to the first rank among states, but for historical reasons have abandoned the traditional badge of great-power status. Neither their defence policies nor their military forces are designed to protect or expand their worldwide interests and influence.

Paradoxes and Perspectives

In the 1970s the two pairs of states were in a paradoxical situation. Britain and France embarked upon the postwar era as restored world powers and conducted their policies accordingly. They set out to develop military capabilities to support their status and responsibilities. This included the acquisition of nuclear weapons. Their starting points and routes were different, but they had reached the same stage. They

The Military Dimension

had become regional powers, caught in the contradictions of trying to balance their nuclear and conventional forces within the context of limited economic resources.

The contradiction was essentially betwen the concepts of deterrence and defence. Within each concept lay a further contradiction. Deterrence was directed against the improbable threat of a Soviet attack, but was also an instrument of persuasion directed to the United States. In that role it fulfilled two functions: to persuade the Americans to accept their status as major powers and to give them preferential treatment accordingly; and to make sure that the American deterrent remained a credible instrument in the defence of Western Europe.

The consequences of these policies were rather different from what was intended. They irritated the Americans, who did not accept their status as equals when dealing with the Soviet Union, and they strengthened pressures in the United States for an American withdrawal from Europe. For the Americans have seen British and French nuclear armament as a dissipation of national resources which should have gone towards improving conventional forces that would be more useful in strengthening the overall defences of the West. In unintentionally promoting such discord, British and French nuclear policies encouraged the Russians in efforts to drive wedges into the Atlantic Alliance, by playing on the differences between the nuclear and non-nuclear weapon states in West Europe, and between the European nuclear powers and the United States.

The conventional forces of Britain and France are designed to represent an earnest of their determination to resist a Soviet attack, and a warning that an armed clash on the continent would very quickly escalate to and beyond the nuclear threshold. Thus, British and French conventional forces in Europe are primarily triggers of nuclear escalation, which would immediately involve the United States.

They are also intended to support operations overseas in defence of residual imperial interests. However, their value as instruments for such purposes or as symbols of great-power status is doubtful, except in the short term. The French, for example, have intervened militarily on several occasions in various successor states of their African empire, although their failure in 1979 to resolve the crisis in Chad is significant. It revealed the limits of their interest and ability to sustain a military intervention in such a situation. Moreover, they invited Nigeria, their chief rival for influence in West Africa, to assume the role of mediator and peace-keeper in that strife-torn country.[27] At the time of writing the French are once again in Chad, but the outcome of their mission remains uncertain.

The British expedition to recapture the Falkland Islands in the spring of 1982 is an even more interesting illustration of various aspects of the problem facing the former imperial powers. It may be seen as one of the last chapters in the long retreat from empire. Successive British governments had hoped to shed this particular legacy of the past, and as a consequence led the Argentinians to believe that they would eventually give up the territories. The decision of Mrs Thatcher's government to scrap the ice-patrol vessel HMS *Endurance* in the interests of economy, positively encouraged an Argentinian *coup de main*, in the belief that Britain would not try to defend its possessions in the South Atlantic.

The Argentinians must have been surprised by the firm and swift response to their invasion. The liberation of the islands was a brilliantly executed operation in the familiar pattern of the days when the Royal Navy ruled the seas: initial humiliation and disaster eventually to be retrieved by the heroic action of numerically inferior but technically and professionally superior forces. But there were important differences between this operation and earlier campaigns, underlining the security problems of former great powers that are not quite reconciled to their new circumstances.

On this occasion it was not just a naval squadron which was sent but most of the navy, with the consequence that its departure left a serious gap in the defences of the Atlantic Alliance. If the Argentinians had waited a further six months or a year before delivering their attack, it is extremely doubtful that Britain would have been in a position to launch the Task Force at all because there would have been insufficient carriers to provide the necessary air cover.

Germany and Japan set out after the war to regain their sovereignty; to become an equal of the other major West European states in the case of Germany; and to achieve a high status among the nations of the world in the case of Japan. Such ambitions would only be realized if they could count on American protection for security against their only potential enemy in the postwar world. In the pursuit of these objectives they emerged as world powers of a new kind, depending primarily on their economic strength. The influence they exercise in international affairs does not depend on their armies, navies and airforces; it depends on their capital reserves, their technology, their managerial skills, their trade and their investments. But it also depends on their close ties to the United States.

The Military Dimension

In the process of acquiring economic strength, they have developed a formidable industrial and technological infrastructure which could be used as a foundation for the production of highly sophisticated armaments, including nuclear weapons and other new military technologies. The Federal Republic is already comfortably among the top ten countries in the league table of arms exporters. Japan occupies a much more modest position due to the government's policy not to permit the export of arms. This is coupled with restrictions on the manufacture of certain kinds of 'offensive' weapons. Japan does, however, produce most of the equipment in use by the SDF, except for certain types of aircraft. Therefore, the ability to manufacture armaments on a large scale and to export them exists in both countries.

The four states are at present under great pressure to increase their defence capabilities and to assume worldwide responsibilities within the context of an emerging global alliance system. The pressure comes from the defence lobbies in each country, which are by no means confined to the military establishments, and from the United States. The course of their military policies and the place of the military instrument in their security policies will be determined by three factors, two of them domestic and one external.

The first domestic factor is the economic environment. Since economic and social welfare are the areas of greatest interest and concern to the population, its attitudes and those of the politicians will be much affected by the course of the current depression and its impact on the standard of living and the rates of unemployment. Strong protectionist pressures are emerging in Europe and America, and if they are successful they will have a frustrating effect on Japan. Trade wars and economic nationalism generally exacerbate nationalist feelings, and it is no coincidence that the sense of crisis in the Atlantic Alliance at the beginning of the 1980s is surfacing at a time of serious economic friction between Europe and America. In such circumstances all those who believe that military force is the decisive argument in international relations are reinforced by calls for increased armaments as a means of stimulating the economy and expanding exports. A heavy emphasis on the need to strengthen defence against a vague Soviet 'threat'; calls for some form of national service in Britain; the pressure from some industrialists in Japan for a lifting of restrictions on arms exports and for consideration of the introduction of conscription — all are straws in the wind.

Alongside these trends one has to set a second factor: a generational change. Everywhere the postwar generation (people who were children or youths before and during the war) is making way for the post-postwar generation (people who were born during or after the war). This new wave, rising more quickly to the top in Western Europe than in Japan, is not affected by great-power status or war guilt. Indeed, they have no experience of war, so they can indulge their fantasies in the enormous popular literature about the last war without deep emotional involvement. Young students in Japan can now talk about the 'inevitability' of Japan acquiring the bomb — an idea abhorrent to their generation twenty-five years ago.

The outlook of the new generation could cut either way. It could mean less preoccupation with the power status of their country, less attachment to its past glories, less belief that it has a mission in the world, less concern to avenge the wrongs of the past. It may, on the other hand, lessen belief in the futility of war, lessen anxieties about its horrors, make the military once more appealing in the drab surroundings of an economic depression and, in the Federal Republic of Germany and Japan, remove inhibitions stemming from a sense of guilt or shame, especially as the world has seen so much brutality committed by the former victor nations since then.

The outcome of the various pulls in the domestic environment will eventually be decided by developments in the international environment and particularly the reactions to the developing relationship between the superpowers. In this respect the relationship with the United States will be most important, and it is that factor which brings us back to the point made at the beginning of the chapter. In the last resort, all four states depend on the United States for their military security against the Soviet Union. Such a statement is, of course, impossible to prove, but it may be a sound assumption in the light of experience since 1945. Soviet advances and domination have been at the expense of countries which have not been included in a defensive system patronized by the United States. The attack on Korea was made because Korea seemed to be placed outside the American defence perimeter. None of the East European states that have fallen under Soviet domination was included in the Western sphere. Afghanistan was a non-aligned buffer state until 1978. Cuba was, of course, within the American sphere, but here, significantly, the revolution came from within; so that it had removed itself from the American camp before the Russians started to build missile bases there.

The Military Dimension

Notes

1. Central Policy Review Staff, *Review of Overseas Representation* (London, HMSO, 1977), p. x, para 5. This document, commonly known as the *Berrill Report*, had the examination of British overseas representation as its remit, but devoted its introduction to a consideration of the basic objectives of British foreign policy, which it did in a sensible, pragmatic, and very British way.
2. Ibid., pp. x-xi, para. 8.
3. Phillip Darby, *British Defence Policy East of Suez 1947-1968* (London, Oxford University Press for The Royal Institute of International Affairs, 1973), p. 20.
4. C.J. Bartlett, *The Long Retreat: A Short History of British Defence Policy, 1945-1970* (London, Macmillan, 1972), p. 30.
5. Ibid., p. 54; William Wallace, *The Foreign Policy Process in Britain* (London, The Royal Institute of International Affairs, 1976), pp. 137-8.
6. Darby, pp. 59-60.
7. Wolf Mendl, *Deterrence and Persuasion: French Nuclear Armament in the Context of National Policy, 1945-1969* (London, Faber & Faber, 1970), pp. 19-21.
8. Margaret Gowing, *Independence and Deterrence: Britain and Atomic Energy, 1945-1952. Vol. I: Policy Making*, pp. 318-21.
9. *The Times*, 24 February 1958.
10. Exchange of letters between Prime Minister Thatcher and President Carter, *Cmd 7979* (London, HMSO, July 1980) and between Mrs Thatcher and President Reagan, *Cmd 8517* (London, HMSO, March 1982).
11. John Simpson, 'Britain's Nuclear Deterrent: The Impending Decisions' (*ADIU Report*, vol. I, no. 1, June 1979).
12. Mendl, *Deterrence and Persuasion*, pp. 55-61.
13. Ibid., pp. 45-6. De Gaulle was especially annoyed by the British failure to follow up the idea of a Franco-British nuclear force, which was aired at the de Gaulle-Macmillan meeting at Rambouillet in December 1962. Edmond Jouve, *Le Général de Gaulle et la construction de l'Europe (1940-1966)* (Paris, Librairie Générale de Droit et de Jurisprudence, R. Pichou & R. Durand-Auziar, 1967), vol. I, p. 181. See also Roger Massip, *De Gaulle et l'Europe* (Paris, Flammarion, 1963), pp. 112-13, 181.
14. P.-M. Gallois, *Stratégie de l'Age Nucléaire* (Paris, Calmann-Lévy, 1960).
15. See for example, Michel Jobert, 'De l'Allemagne', *Politique Etrangère*, no. 1, 1979, pp. 7-19. The Treaty of Rapallo, a treaty of friendship and commerce, was signed unexpectedly between Germany and Russia in 1922 during an international conference on economic questions and reparations, one of whose objectives had been the normalization of relations between Russia and its wartime allies. It broke down over the question of repudiated Russian debts. The Russo-German *rapprochement*, therefore, came as a shock to the allies. They would have been more than shocked at the time if they had known that it included secret provisions for the training of German officers in Russia in the management of weapons forbidden by the treaty of Versailles.
16. Bartlett, p. 106.
17. Darby, pp. 141-2.
18. Bartlett, pp. 95-9.
19. Ibid., pp. 125-6.
20. See Articles 4, 6, 10, 12 of 'Proclamation to Japan', 26 July 1945. *The Department of State Bulletin*, Vol. XIII No. 318, 29 July 1945, p. 137.
21. 'We hereby undertake for the Emperor, the Japanese Government *and*

54 *The Military Dimension*

their successors to carry out the provisions of the Potsdam Declaration . . . ' (my italics). Hugh Borton, *Japan's Modern Century* (New York, The Ronald Press Company, 1955), pp. 487-8.

22. Roger Buckley, *Occupation Diplomacy: Britain, the United States and Japan: 1945-1952* (Cambridge University Press, 1982).

23. 'Subjective civilian control achieves its end by civilianizing the military, making them the mirror of the state. Objective civilian control achieves its end by militarizing the military, making them the tool of the state.' Samuel P. Huntington, *The Soldier and the State: The Theory and Politics of Civil-Military Relations* (New York, Random House, 1964), p.83. For a general discussion of the concept see ibid., pp. 83-96.

24. 'Artikel 26:

(1) Handlungen die geeignet sind und in der Absicht vorgenommen werden, das friedliche Zusammenleben der Völker zu stören, insbesondere die Führung eines Angriffskrieges vorzubereiten, sind verfassungswidrig. Sie sind unter Strafe zu stellen.

(2) Zur Kriegsführung bestimmte Waffen dürfen nur mit Genehmigung der Bundesregierung hergestellt, befördert und in Verkehr gebracht werden. Das Nähere regelt ein Bundesgesetz.'

Grundgesetz für die Bundesrepublik Deutschland (Hagen, Pick-Verlag, 1949), p. 9.

25. Protocol No. III on the Control of Armaments, Part I, Annexes 1-3 (*Documents Agreed on by the Conference of Ministers held in Paris, October 20-23, 1954*, Cmd 9304, Miscellaneous No. 32 (1954), London, HMSO), pp. 39-43. See also Catherine McArdle Kelleher, *Germany and the Politics of Nuclear Weapons* (New York and London, Columbia University Press, 1975).

26. See, for instance, John E. Endicott, *Japan's Nuclear Option: Political, Technical and Strategic Factors* (New York, Praeger Publishers, 1975).

27. In the end the Nigerians fared no better. For a discussion of the problem of Chad see F.O. Adisa, *The Development of Nigeria's Defence Policy: 1960-1979*, Chapter 6 (unpublished Ph.D Thesis, University of London, 1983).

3 THE ALLIANCE WITH THE UNITED STATES

> We've heard a lot of protests from our European allies. I'm sorry. The United States is the leader of the free world and under this administration we are beginning once again to act like it.[1]

At the beginning of the 1980s the official American argument ran roughly along the following lines: the threat from the Soviet Union is 'real' because of its greatly increased military capabilities. Unless it is checked it will lead to a Russian-imposed world order. The United States can no longer meet the challenge on its own, but has to work in close association with Europe and Japan. This implies the development of a global strategy for the West, not only to contain the Soviet Union, but also to assist the Third World in order to prevent further Russian advances in those regions.

The allies of the United States faced several problems in formulating their response to the explicit and implicit American demands to accept both the diagnosis and the prescription. If one looks back over the history of the postwar years, can one say it was likely that the United States would stick to this view indefinitely? The historical evidence points to the opposite conclusion. Periods of American militancy have alternated with periods dominated by the search for accommodation with the Soviet Union. Was the Soviet threat so serious and was there a danger that the military balance might tip decisively in Russia's favour? What was the evidence for Russia's aggressive and expansionist designs? Was it not simply opportunist, exploiting what openings there were, and otherwise being cautious and defensive? It could at least be argued that much of what passed for expansion was motivated as much by an obsessive concern for the real or imagined requirements of security.

What was the link between containment of the Soviet Union and assistance of the Third World? It could be that Western activities in the countries of those regions presented the Russians with precisely the opportunities they were designed to prevent. Finally, and most important, to what extend did the friends of the United States share this particular analysis of trends in world politics, and were they prepared to go along with the remedies proposed? Were they in the interests of the allies, and were they likely to achieve their objectives?

55

For each of its major Western associates the security relationship with the United States has so far fulfilled two distinct functions. It provided the necessary protection against possible Soviet threats and pressures and, ironically, it was also an instrument for the pursuit of national policies, independently of the United States and sometimes in conflict with American interests.

This was all very well as long as the United States felt secure in its dominant position among the Western states and in its strategic superiority over the Soviet Union. Western criticisms of and reservations about supporting its policies in Vietnam might have been irritating, but they could be tolerated. When France withdrew from the integrated structure of the Atlantic Alliance in 1966, it posed a serious threat to the Alliance's efficiency, especially of its logistical network, but President Johnson could rest assured that France would still fight alongside its allies.[2]

Things are changed now. The Americans maintain a teetering equilibrium with the Soviet Union, and see themselves as being overtaken in certain military fields. They want their allies to help redress the balance. The United States's dominance in the Western world remains unchallenged and is likely to persist as long as each of the major states acts primarily on its own account. From the earliest days of NATO, American military aid has always been given through *bilateral* agreements, in contrast to the Canadian practice which was to operate through the Standing Group in Washington and to follow the recommendations of the Secretariat.[3] Bilateral arrangements obviously suited the interests and ambitions of the individual allies, but they also provided the United States with a more effective leverage over their policies.

Some decline in American military power *vis-à-vis* the Soviet Union and economic weakness *vis-à-vis* at least some of the allies, raises questions about the continued effectiveness of the alliance structures and whether they can be adapted to changing circumstances, or whether new structures should be created to accommodate changing relationships among the Western powers. On the surface it would appear that one has to consider only two existing alliance systems: the multilateral system of the North Atlantic Alliance and the bilateral system of the Japan-United States Mutual Security Treaty. In fact, however, each of the three West European states has a distinctive alliance relationship with the United States within the North Atlantic system.

The Alliance with the United States

Security Treaties and Relationships

The North Atlantic Treaty (see Appendix I) has acquired an aura of permanence after three decades, and there is nothing that suggests that it is in immediate danger of disintegration, in spite of many strains and obvious differences among the allies. Some of its provisions, however, contain the seeds of serious dissensions, and others the possibility of a redefinition of its objectives. The international environment in which it came into existence has long since changed, but not its primary purpose: a defensive alliance directed against Soviet expansion in Europe. Recent disagreements over nuclear strategy, especially between the smaller members of the Alliance and the more powerful members, and the resurrection of an anti-nuclear movement with neutralist overtones, this time more widely spread over Western Europe, are not likely to undermine the still more widely spread acceptance of the necessity of some kind of collective security system underwritten by the United States.

In terms of legal obligations, however, the Treaty does allow considerable latitude to its members, giving it the character of a traditional alliance despite an unprecedented degree of military integration in peacetime. In Article 5 of the Treaty all the parties accept that an attack on one of them is an attack on all, and pledge themselves to come to the assistance of the victim, each member state taking 'such action as it deems necessary, including the use of armed force, to restore and maintain the security of the North Atlantic area.' Hence, a very considerable degree of discretion rests with each government, especially in the event of an ambiguous Soviet move.[4] How, for example, could one be sure that the incursion of a Russian patrol, aircraft or ship into allied territory was the prelude to a deliberate act of aggression and not an accident or a response to some sort of perceived local provocation? It is easy to imagine governments interpreting the incident differently, especially when the circumstances were unclear, as they usually are in military operations of any kind. Their interpretations are also bound to reflect the political preoccupations of the moment.

The Soviets probably have no intention of testing the cohesion of the Alliance in this way, but a much more immediate and divisive problem has arisen since the Soviet invasion of Afghanistan. Article 6, suitably amended since the accession of Greece and Turkey in 1952, and to take note of Algerian independence in 1962, defines the territorial limit of the Treaty. Apart from the territories of the parties in Europe and North America, its scope includes 'the Mediterranean Sea or the North Atlantic area north of the Tropic of Cancer.' Moves are now afoot to widen the range of allied responsibilities to counter the global operations of the Soviet Union, especially in the Middle East and the Gulf region and still more recently in the Caribbean and Central America. Such proposals, however, are meeting very strong resistance, particularly from members on the European continent. The Europeans have shown themselves willing to join in non-military measures to signal their displeasure to the Soviet Union, but are reluctant to contemplate military action of any kind for various reasons which I will discuss later.

So much for some areas of friction which could have a deleterious effect on the functioning of the Alliance. The possibilities for change and adjustment exist in the provision for Treaty review at any time after 1959 (Article 12) and in the escape clause for any disgruntled member state, which is free to terminate its membership after giving a year's notice (Article 13). This has been in operation since 1969, and in spite of withdrawals from the integrated military structure by France and Greece, no member has so far taken advantage of the provisions of Article 13.

Within the context of an alliance which no government wants to dissolve, or at least to leave, each of the three leading European members pursues its own 'special' relationship with the United States, often at the expense of other allies.

For a long time the British have fancied themselves as privileged partners of the United States, and since this fitted in with concepts of their own role and that of the US in Europe, they have always put the interests of the 'special relationship' ahead of their other commitments. There has also been, it is true, an anti-mainstream tendency, which has been either strongly pro-European or neutralist. The interesting thing is that these tendencies have been much stronger in the two major parties when they were in opposition than in office. Thus, the Conservatives have shown themselves more enthusiastic for Europe in opposition than in office, with the exception of the Heath government of 1970-4. Similarly, the Labour Party has leaned towards neutralist and 'Little Englander' policies when out of office. In government, however, the Labour Party has, if anything, been even more enthusiastic about the American connection than have the Conservatives, a characteristic especially marked under Harold Wilson's premiership.

The result of more than three decades of British policy is a low reputation in Europe and a declining influence in Washington, notwithstanding close personal relationships between some British Prime

The Alliance with the United States

Ministers and American Presidents (Macmillan-Kennedy, Callaghan-Carter, Thatcher-Reagan). Suez 1956 should have taught the British that the United States will not support its ally in all circumstances. The so-called 'special relationship' is no longer a policy option. The problem for Britain is its place in Europe and in the dialogue between the United States and its major industrialized partners.

It has been said of the Federal Republic of Germany that

> she staked the achievement of her military and political influence not on a privileged bilateral partnership with the United States or on an independent nuclear programme but on the tight military and political integration of the alliance ... [5]

The nature of the German relationship with the United States has been the opposite to the one which Britain tried to cultivate. The British have always tried to impress on the United States their unique importance, and claimed the status of a privileged partner. The reverse was true of the German-American relationship.

Following the outbreak of the war in Korea, the United States pressed strongly for German rearmament, originally within the context of NATO, but allowed itself to be convinced that it should take place within a European Defence Community (EDC). When this initiative began to falter, Secretary of State Dulles tried to put pressure on the French to ratify EDC by threatening an 'agonizing reappraisal' of the American commitment to Europe. After the EDC was finally rejected by the French National Assembly, it was largely due to Anthony Eden's skilful diplomacy that a solution was found in the Paris and London Agreements of the autumn of 1954. The Brussels Treaty Organisation was converted into Western European Union (WEU) with the addition of Germany and Italy; the Federal Republic of Germany was admitted to NATO with a commitment to supply the same number of troops that had been stipulated under EDC; German armament was to be controlled by WEU and the ban on certain categories of weapons, such as guided missiles, long-range bombers, large warships, could be waived only at the request of the Supreme Commander Allied Forces in Europe (SACEUR) with the approval of two thirds of the WEU Council.

The United States had thus got what it wanted in the face of considerable misgivings among the Federal Republic's neighbours and a general feeling of hostility or indifference within the Federal Republic itself. Chancellor Adenauer, however, had accepted and supported

German rearmament as part of his overall strategy to regain national sovereignty through full integration into the Western Alliance. This would give the German Federal Republic the security guarantee it needed and useful diplomatic leverage in future dealings with the United States and the Soviet Union.[6]

Henceforth, successive German Federal governments were to exploit their country's dependence on American protection and its position as the keystone of the Western Alliance in order to secure the objectives of their policies. Unlike the Anglo-American relationship in which there was a senior partner and a junior partner whose roles never changed, the American-German relationship was only in appearance one between senior and junior partners, for the Americans felt as dependent on the Federal Republic in pursuit of their European polices as vice versa.

The Multilateral Force (MLF) was a good example of this characteristic of the relationship. First brought up in the autumn of 1960, it was intended partly to sabotage de Gaulle's idea of a 'Directorate of Three' in NATO,[7] partly to deal with the problem of nuclear proliferation within the Alliance, and to bring the British and incipient French nuclear forces under some sort of American control, and largely to stifle a German demand for a 'finger on the trigger'. Although the MLF was eventually sabotaged in its turn by Harold Wilson's Atlantic Nuclear Force (ANF), the history of the debate illustrates American sensitivity to real or imagined German demands.

The two nations have been locked into a relationship which has enabled the Germans to use it as an instrument with which to enhance their status in the Alliance, to manage their relations with the French, and to pursue their Ostpolitik, taking care never to get out of step with the United States in too great a measure. The most recent example of the central importance of the Federal Republic of Germany, both to the United States and the Alliance, has been Chancellor Schmidt's successful insistence that the Pershing II and cruise-launched missiles could be stationed on German soil only if other European members of the Alliance accepted them as well.

France, just as much as Britain and Germany, depends on the European commitment of the United States for its basic security, and it would be a mistake to read into the stormy and sometimes acrimonious passages of the postwar relationship with America a failure to appreciate this fact. Whereas the British hoped to ingratiate themselves with the Americans on the basis of cultural affinity and wartime associations, and the Germans managed their relationship on the basis of mutual dependence, the French did so by pushing their nuisance value

The Alliance with the United States

to the utmost, always taking care not to strain American tolerance to breaking point.

After they had left the integrated structure of the Alliance, they not only remained firm in their basic commitment to it, but continued to co-operate unofficially in a variety of ways. The Gaullist period (1958-69) saw the most extreme manifestations of French 'independence', coloured by the General's personal animus and his exalted conception of France, but even he took care to leave no doubt where he stood on the central issues of the East-West confrontation, as demonstrated by his strong support for the United States over Cuba in 1962. His attacks against the Americans were directed at any sign of domination, and attempts to force France to accept policies without full consultation and participation in the policy-making. Hence, French opposition to arms-control agreements, which were regarded as instruments confirming the hegemony of the superpowers; the refusal to support the Americans over Vietnam, seen as a misreading of the true state of affairs in that region; and resistance to any measures which seemed to consolidate American control over the Alliance.

In recent years there has been a lessening of French opposition to the Americans, although some of the old reflexes were in evidence over the Iran and Afghanistan crises. None the less, the French position has been basically aligned with that of its European partners. This is more a sign of recognition that the Europeans can and do act independently than a return to an acceptance of American leadership.

From the record of the past three decades there emerges a picture of the three major West European states as members of a multilateral alliance, but each having a special relationship with the United States, whose purpose was to combine the security which could only be provided by the Americans with the pursuit of particular national objectives. Each took a special course, and until recently their policies were not strongly linked by common objectives. It may be that the events since the autumn of 1979 will turn out to have been an important landmark in the evolution of a common West European position over relations with the United States.

The position of Japan has, of course, been quite different. From the beginning it has been firmly embedded in a bilateral security relationship with the United States, whose terms are laid down in the revised Treaty of Mutual Cooperation and Security of 1960 (see Appendix II). Unlike the North Atlantic Treaty, by which all the member states are bound to regard aggression against one of their number as aggression against all, this treaty pledges mutual assistance only in the event of an attack against either party 'in the territories under the administration of Japan' (Article V). In the event of an attack on the United States or on American armed forces elsewhere in the world, Japan is under no obligation to come to its assistance. It can be maintained, however, that under the terms of Article IV, Japan has some moral obligation to take note of threats to peace and security within the East Asian region outside its territory. Moreover, there is an even greater commitment in Article VI in which Japan grants the United States the use of bases 'For the purpose of contributing to the security of Japan and the maintenance of international peace and security in the Far East'.

An exchange of letters between Prime Minister Kishi and Secretary of State Herter, clarifying the use of American bases in Japan 'for military combat operations other than those conducted under Article V', gives Japan a kind of veto right through the requirement of 'prior consultation'. In a subsequent communiqué, President Eisenhower further strengthened Japan's rights by assuring Kishi 'that the United States has no intention of acting in a manner contrary to the wishes of the Japanese Government with respect to matters involving prior consultation under the treaty.'[8] Article VI and these agreements had a double effect: they have provided the basis on which the United States and those in Japan who share its view urge Japan to interpret more broadly its responsibilities as an ally, and they have been the basis on which the Japanese government has been able to uphold its strictly limited obligations and make sure that Japan is not drawn into America's quarrels elsewhere.

The postwar objectives of Japan were essentially the same as those of the Federal Republic of Germany: economic and social reconstruction, rehabilitation in the international community, restoration to a position of importance and influence. The main instrument for the achievement of these objectives was the security relationship with the United States, and each country exploited its position as an important and indispensable ally. The main difference was that the route of West Germany's rehabilitation lay through rearmament within the Atlantic Alliance, whereas the Japanese rearmed as slowly as they could, and based their rise to influence on economic growth.

Given the direction of American policy since the war, one should have thought that the Federal Republic of Germany had turned out to be a more acceptable and welcome ally than Japan. In fact, it has not been so. Both are considered to be important allies and their strength as a welcome reinforcement for the West, but the strategic importance of the Germans has been a source of as much friction with the United

The Alliance with the United States

States as the economic power of Japan.

In spite of the obvious differences between a multilateral security treaty in which all the members share equal responsibilities, at least in theory, and a bilateral security treaty in which there is no equal obligation and the main defence burden is explicitly borne by one of the parties, there are also significant common features in the security relationships of the West European states and Japan with the United States. In both treaties there is provision, usual in treaties of this kind, for termination of membership after a year's notice (Article X of the US-Japan Treaty, operative since 1970), but what is far more remarkable is their durability, and that after three decades of existence — the span of one generation — there is little outward sign of their collapse or disintegration. They are almost regarded as permanent features of the international landscape.

The United States is clearly the dominant member of both alliances, but there are limits in each treaty on the extent to which the other allies are committed to support it (Articles V in both pacts). These safeguards are strongly reinforced by the geographical limitations written into both treaties.

It has been said that two basically different conceptions of the objective of the Atlantic Alliance were held in the United States at the time of its inception.[9] One was that of George Kennan, who saw it as a political guarantee extended to Western Europe; a kind of protective mantle under which it could recover and from a position of strength eventually negotiate an all-European settlement with the Soviet Union. This also seemed to be the conception of General de Gaulle. The other was held by Presidents Truman and Eisenhower, and envisaged a strong and united Europe, nurtured and protected by the United States, which would be closely tied to the US within the Atlantic Community. This view was also shared by Chancellor Adenauer.

The same duality of purpose may be detected from the start in the security relationship between the United States and Japan, although the differences were between Americans and Japanese and not between one group of American leaders and another. From the time that they changed course in their occupation policy, the American objective was to foster the economic recovery of Japan so that it would become an important link in the chain of alliances that was in the process of being forged. In this way the United States would not only be able to control Japan, but would gain its support in the task of containing the communist bloc. While the Japanese leaders shared the American perception of a communist threat, they also saw the special relationship with the United States as a means whereby to regain their independence and eventually to develop their own policies, especially towards China. The aim to avoid too close an identification with American policy is well illustrated by the attitude towards the China problem in the negotiations leading up to the Treaty of San Francisco in 1951.[10]

Contemporary Problems

In spite of the different origins and circumstances of their security relationships with the United States, West Europeans and Japanese face the same basic problems today. The similarity in their positions arises from changed perceptions of the international environment and the experience of their relations with the United States over the past ten years. They make it both meaningful and necessary that Europeans and Japanese cease thinking about their association with the United States in isolation from each other.

Following the Cold War of the 1940s and 1950s, there came a period of equilibrium in which it was fashionable to talk about a limited-adversary relationship between the superpowers and the emergence of a multipolar system of power. From there it was a natural progression to the idea of regionalism as the focus of international security. In each region local powers were seen as potential contestants for hegemony (Japan and China in East Asia, India and Pakistan in South Asia, Saudi Arabia and Iran in the Gulf area, Argentina and Brazil in Latin America, and so on), with the Soviet Union taking what advantage it could from local conflicts to expand its influence without, however, seriously threatening to upset the superpower balance.

In the middle of the 1970s the international climate began to change once more. This coincided with the change from a Republican to a Democratic Administration in the United States. It is one of the ironies of recent history that an administration that was swept to power on a popular mood against the cynical domestic and foreign politics of its predecessor and was initially sustained by the idealism which is one of the traits of American populism, should, within a couple of years or so, preside over a marked deterioration of relations with the Soviet Union. One reason for this turn of events was the generally incompetent handling of foreign affairs.

There was no lack of ideas, and in one important respect, human rights, the Carter Administration continued the policy of linkage that had been one of the principal guidelines in America's approach to the

Soviet Union in the Nixon/Kissinger era.[11] The only trouble was that it was handled in such a way that it left the Russians bewildered and confused.

In his relations with West Europe and Japan, President Carter also failed to live up to his ideals. America's partners had become increasingly uneasy over the policies of the previous Administration. The Japanese had been given three minutes' warning of the historic announcement of Nixon's impending visit to China, and were justified in thinking that the Chinese colossus played a much greater part in Kissinger's *Weltanschauung* than their own country. The Europeans, too, suspected that they were no more than subordinate though important pieces in the grand game of international chess. The SALT process was not only conducted over their heads, but was also seen as furthering an emerging superpower condominium.

The new President's Special Adviser for National Security Affairs, Zbigniew Brzezinski, had been one of the architects of trilateralism, and the Democratic Administration was dedicated to putting the trilateral partnership into the forefront of American policy, in contrast to the triangular power system (US, USSR, China) which had been at the centre of Kissinger's foreign policy. However, the high hopes of the allies for a change in the emphasis of American policy under Carter and a greater regard for their interests and feelings were soon dashed.

In keeping with his election promise, Carter announced his decision to withdraw American ground forces from Korea, without any pretence at consulting the Japanese. Although the withdrawal was later postponed indefinitely, there were to be other examples during the Iranian and Afghan crises of the American penchant to act first and consult afterwards. Japanese susceptibilities were also ruffled by repeated lectures on the need to increase defence spending. Privately, many of the conservative politicians shared the American concern for a militarily stronger Japan, but there was more than a touch of playing to the gallery when Foreign Minister Ito told the Upper House Committee for Foreign Affairs immediately after the election of President Reagan that 'Japan's basic attitude towards increasing its defence capability will not change whoever takes over the US administration. Japan's defence is an issue about which Japan should make decisions on its own initiative.'[12]

The Europeans fared no better. First there was the handling of the Enhanced Radiation Weapon (neutron bomb) issue, a matter of literally vital concern to the Europeans and particularly the Germans. Although Chancellor Schmidt had been sympathetic to the development of this weapon, the President's insistence on direct European participation in the decision to go ahead with production had created such strong political reactions in Europe that he was deeply embarrassed by the subsequent uproar.[13] Further problems arose over the SALT negotiations with their bearing on the theatre nuclear balance. Erratic American behaviour during the crises at the end of 1979 created more irritation. When he left office, President Carter's personal relations with his principal European ally, Helmut Schmidt, could hardly have been worse.

By the time of President Reagan's inauguration, the European states and Japan had been through a decade in which it seemed that they had been either ignored by successive American administrations, or regarded as junior partners whose job it was to fall in with whatever the American design might be. The unease and wariness with which they greeted the newly elected Republican Administration were due partly to the experience of the past and partly to the unknown calibre of the new American leaders. They also stemmed from an awareness that apprehensions about the Soviet threat were leading the United States to reassess relationships with its allies.

Since the Russian invasion of Afghanistan and to some extent even before, there has been a subtle shift in the American concept of regionalism and of the role of the United States in underwriting the various security systems that had sprung up in the previous thirty years.

Hitherto, the prevailing view of a polycentric world had been dominated by the idea that new regional centres of power and influence were emerging under the over-arching superpower relationship which was governed by its own system of checks and balances. The United States might be allied to some of these regional powers, but such alliances were more or less self-contained within the particular region. While the emphasis on regional security systems has continued, they have acquired a new dimension since the end of the 1970s. Attention has shifted from intra-regional balances (China-Japan, India-Pakistan, and so on) to the link between these balances and the global balance which appears to be threatened by a new Soviet expansionism.

For the Americans, relations between China and Japan have become an element in the containment of the Soviet Union in North-east Asia. The balance between ASEAN and a Vietnam-dominated Indochina is seen as helping to contain Soviet influence in that region. Relations between India and Pakistan and among the Gulf states are related to the problem of countering the Russian presence in the Indian Ocean. American intervention in the regional politics of the Middle East and

Central America are guided by the overriding objective of keeping the Soviets out of these areas, or at least at bay. Countering Russian influence is a key factor of American policy in each region. The Russians, with their concern over superpower status and ideological commitments, see their relations with various states around the world in the same light, so that there has been a movement towards the establishment of two competing *global* alliance systems; the one led by the United States, the other by the Soviet Union. This was a new departure in international politics at the end of the 1970s.

In the previous two-and-a-half decades the United States had expected to shoulder the global burden of Western defence, with some assistance from the British until the late 1960s. The British withdrawal from east of Suez was a long protracted process,[14] due partly to pressures from the United States and the Commonwealth countries in South-east Asia, which wanted a British presence to remain in that region and in the Indian Ocean. The Americans were fully occupied in Vietnam, but their reluctance to see the British go was not primarily because they felt that they could not manage without British military support — they had no hesitation in replacing the French as a military power in Indochina — but because they saw political benefits from the presence of another Western power in the region, one which had special ties with some of the local governments.

While the Americans were ready to assume the functions of global policeman, with or without the assistance of Britain, they urged their friends to assume a greater responsibility for defence in their own regions. It was axiomatic, however, that the United States would back up the local states through its nuclear, naval and air power, and even with substantial ground forces where necessary. What was new in the 1970s was the growing power and self-confidence of some of America's allies, and the feeling that the United States could no longer carry the full responsibility for a global containment policy which had acquired a new urgency in the face of Soviet military expansion.

The first formal expression of the policy of shifting more of the burden of security on to the shoulders of the allies came in the summer of 1969 with the 'Nixon Doctrine', which was elaborated under the impact of the Vietnam War and was addressed to America's Asian allies.[15] The United States undertook to keep its treaty commitments, and would act as a shield against any threat from a nuclear power to an ally or 'a nation whose survival we consider vital to our security and the security of the region as a whole.' It would 'furnish military and economic assistance when requested and as appropriate', but stressed that a nation directly threatened should accept *primary* responsibility for its security and for providing manpower for its defence.

In the early 1980s the main difference between the strategic conceptions of the United States and its principal associates is over the relationship between regional and global security. For the West Europeans and Japanese, with the British occupying a position somewhere between them and the Americans, military security is a regional or local matter, the willingness to deploy and use armed forces being in direct proportion to perceptions of 'vital national interests'. For France such interests may extend to parts of Africa; for the Federal Republic of Germany not much beyond the Central Front and Northern Flank of NATO. Japan, under American pressure, has extended the definition from the confines of territorial waters to the sea approaches up to a thousand miles from the shoreline.

Americans, on the other hand, have lately stressed the indivisible whole of Western security. They want the participation of Europeans and Japanese in a global security system. Support is sought for *both* political and military reasons. In the first place, the United States expects its allies to shoulder the main burden of their own defence, thus freeing American forces for service elsewhere. Secondly, they want the allies to provide much more positive diplomatic and economic support in the world at large and at least a token military presence in certain key areas, such as the Gulf, where Western interests appear to be directly threatened.

Differences between the United States and its friends over Western strategy are influenced to some extent by a general crisis in the Western World, caused by the economic depression and the accompanying strains in allied relationships. They also reflect differing appreciations of the nature and extent of the Soviet threat.

Discussion of this issue is at three levels, though they cannot always be clearly separated, and in practice the debate leads to much overlap and a good deal of confusion. At the basic level is the central strategic relationship between the superpowers. The second level is that of the regional military balance in Europe and North-east Asia. At the third level lies a consideration of Soviet policy in the Third World and especially the importance of its military dimension. The first two will be dealt with in the following sections. Soviet policy in the Third World is the subject of Chapters 4 and 5.

The Central Strategic Balance

The question as to what extent American military power has really declined in relation to that of the Soviet Union is not easy to answer. Even if one can disentangle the special pleading of various interest-groups, such as the military establishment or the armament industry, from the argument, one is left with the formidable task of establishing the criteria on which a reasonably objective assessment can be made. There is in addition the problem of judging the effectiveness of Russian military strength, given the closed nature and secretiveness of the Soviet system.

Military balances are affected by the long lead-times between the conception of a new weapons system and its full-scale production. A decision may be taken to develop a new weapon, but there could be a delay of seven or ten years before it is fully operational. Therefore, a balance has to be assessed from both a short-term point of view — what is in place — and a long-term perspective — what is in the pipeline from blueprint to production.

The other major complication in making reliable assessments is that of fixing the relative significance of the criteria that are used. For instance, what weight is to be attached to numbers of men and machines as against the skill and morale of the armed forces? To what extent are geographical factors decisive in assessing the opponent's capability? How sure can one be that the most sophisticated weapon system will function as intended?[16]

Bearing all this in mind, one can see that the fundamental issue of the debate in Europe and Japan has not been whether the states in those regions can provide for their security *without* the United States, but whether the United States would be able and willing to continue providing the same kind of security that it provided in the past as a consequence of its technological, nuclear and naval superiority over the Soviet Union.

In the first two decades after the war the arms race between the superpowers was characterized by the commanding lead of the Americans, which the Russians constantly tried to narrow. Each major development in weapons technology was initiated by the Americans. The Russians were the first in space with the launching of *Sputnik* in 1957, arousing fears of a missile gap in the West, but in fact they did not seriously undermine American superiority.

From the middle of the 1960s onwards, however, they began to catch up in both nuclear and naval armament. By 1970 they had more inter-continental ballistic missile (ICBM) launchers than the Americans, and in 1974 the same was true of submarine-launched ballistic missile (SLBM) launchers. Soviet conventional capability also acquired a new dimension in the 1970s with the development of a long-range naval force. The drive to make the Soviet Union a *global* naval power had started before the Cuban missile crisis of 1962 and before Mr Brezhnev came to power in 1964. In the mid-1950s the Russians had begun to build major surface ships and submarines with the capability of attacking American aircraft carriers. After the United States had launched the first Polaris submarine in 1960, the Soviet Union followed suit, and its first ballistic-missile nuclear submarine (SSBN) was deployed in 1967. Within ten years the SSBN had formed the nucleus of the Russian navy, and the main task of the surface fleet was anti-submarine warfare (ASW).

The experience of the Cuban missile crisis, when the Soviet Union was unable to provide naval protection for its merchant vessels, gave a spurt to the construction of a surface fleet capable of operating at great distances from its Russian bases. The surface strength of the Russian navy (sea-control forces) fulfills three functions: ASW, the protection of the SSBN, and the projection of Soviet power around the world. The commissioning in 1980 of the 25,000 ton *Kirov*, a nuclear-powered missile cruiser and the first capital ship to be built by any navy for many years, reinforced this last function.[17]

While the Russians steadily strengthened and expanded their overall military capabilities, the reverse appeared to be true of the Americans. The Kennedy strategy in the early 1960s of being able to fight 'two and a half' wars (two major conflicts, for example in Europe and East Asia, and a minor guerrilla-type or brush-fire war elsewhere) was reduced to a 'one-and-a-half' wars strategy by 1970. Throughout the decade of the 1970s American policy was affected by the material and moral exhaustion of the Vietnam war. Soviet advances in Africa were not seriously challenged, and everywhere the United States seemed to be in retreat. The American concept of deterrence, which in the 1950s and 1960s had been based on the assumption of a margin of superiority in the central strategic balance, was readapted to the conditions of a rough *equivalence* in nuclear strategic forces, and was embodied in the doctrine of Mutual Assured Destruction (MAD).

The deteriorating relationship between the superpowers in the late 1970s was influenced by the introduction of new and the improvement of existing Soviet weapons systems and by the appearance of Russian warships in the oceans of the world. This aroused fears that equivalence might soon be replaced by a margin of Soviet superiority. Such anxieties were eagerly seized upon and fanned by the defence lobby and its academic and journalist apologists, who had never been reconciled to the idea of equivalence. The inevitable reaction against the post-Vietnam mood of self-doubt, a rare and never very long-lasting phenomenon of the American psyche, further prepared the ground for the return of an administration pledged to redress the shaky balance and make America strong again.

There can be no doubt that Russian military power has grown substantially, both quantitatively and qualitatively, and that there are serious weaknesses in America's defences.[18] Yet in spite of these factors there is equally no doubt that basic strategic parity continues to subsist and can be expected to last for two fundamental reasons. The first is that the comparison of Soviet strength with American weakness is only part of the equation, and that a more realistic assessment must read: American strengths + weaknesses = Soviet strengths + weaknesses. Russia's weaknesses encompass its military technology, economy and the problems of policing its empire.[19] The second reason is that notwithstanding the technological advances made by either side, each disposes of such massive and secure second-strike capabilities, that however potent the opponent's first strike might be, he cannot escape the risk of a mutual holocaust.

Regional Balances

As indicated in Chapter 1 (pp. 22-3), a straightforward comparison of ground and air forces in place in Europe, as illustrated in Table 3.1, would give the Soviet Union a very substantial advantage if the American component were to be withdrawn from the Western side. The only significant Western European superiority appears to be in anti-aircraft guns and armed helicopters. But even with the participation of the US, the Soviet bloc has several advantages.

The standing forces of the Warsaw Pact outnumber those of the Atlantic Alliance (including France) in the northern and central sectors. The inclusion of forces in southern Europe gives the West, even without the American component, a marginal superiority in the number of troops on the ground. However, it is as well to remember that the armies of Greece and Turkey face each other as much as a common foe. The reliability and fighting quality of the non-Russian forces of the Pact are unknown factors. Indeed, recent events in Poland have again underlined the fact that the Soviet forces in Eastern Europe perform the

Table 3.1: NATO and Warsaw Pact Ground and Air Forces in Place in Europe (Excluding the Territory of the USSR), July 1983

Category	NATO (Less US) N. Europe[b]	S. Europe[c]	US	Total	USSR	Non-Soviet Pact	Total
Ground Forces (000)[a]	853	911	222	1,986	871[d]	843	1,714
Ground Force Equipment							
Main battle tanks	8,097	7,625	5,000	20,722	13,000[d]	12,490	25,490
Artillery, multiple rocket launchers	4,228	4,206	562	8,996	5,000[d]	6,830	11,830
Surface-to-surface missile launchers	96	60	144	300	272	335	607
Anti-tank guns	850	96	0	946	678	1,250[d]	1,928
Anti-tank guided weapon launchers	880[d]	500[d]	700	2,080	287	1,500[d]	1,787
Surface-to-air missile launchers (SAM)							
Anti-aircraft guns	1,571	352	180	2,103	1,751[d]	1,400[d]	3,151
	4,355	1,587[d]	120	6,062	1,086[d]	2,900[d]	3,986
Land Attack Aircraft and Fighters							
Bombers	34	0	0	34	455	0	455
Ground-attack fighters	1,120	568	498	2,186	1,100[d]	568	1,668
Fighters	116	0	96	212	700[d]	0	700
Interceptors	416	231	0	647	2,880[d]	1,506	4,386
Reconnaissance[e]	190	98	66	354	400[d]	164	564
Armed helicopters	805	60	330[d]	1,195	700	86	786

Notes: a. Those within the USSR include only those in the Kola Peninsula facing Norway and in the Trans-Caucasus facing Turkey.
b. Includes Canadian and French forces in Europe, but not Spanish forces.
c. Italy, Greece, Turkey.
d. Estimated figures.
e. Includes Early Warning/Electronic Counter-measures Aircraft.

Source: Adapted from *The Military Balance 1983-1984* (London, The International Institute for Strategic Studies, Autumn 1983), pp. 138-9.

dual functions of a front-line force against NATO and an army of occupation.

The comparison of battle tanks reveals an enormous superiority of the Warsaw Pact over NATO on the central and northern fronts. Although the NATO forces are generally superior in quality, that advantage is being eroded with the deployment of the Soviet Union's T-72 tank. NATO's inferiority in the overall number of tactical aircraft on all fronts is balanced by the higher proportion of multi-purpose aircraft, the sophistication of electronic equipment, and its Airborne Warning and Control System (AWACS).

In addition, there are a number of unquantifiable factors, such as morale, technical skill and equipment sophistication, some of which help to redress the balance for the West. Others, such as standardization of equipment, favour the Warsaw Pact.

The problem of logistics is a major source of weakness. It involves safeguarding the sea routes across the Atlantic and the speedy concentration of troops and matériel in the areas of greatest danger. Assuming that the conflict is on the Central European front, the deployment would be across the lines of communications of the front-line formations if France were to deny the passage of reinforcements across its territory. It seems most unlikely that France would or could stand aside in the event of a major conflict in Central Europe, so that this problem is not a serious one. Much more doubtful is the capacity of the allies to bring up their reinforcements in time and in sufficient strength to halt a determined Soviet advance. The activities of Russian submarines, the speed of the Russian advance, and the possibility of a nuclear attack on allied ports and centres of communications might cut the supply lines and overwhelm the initial resistance. There is also the prospect of chaos and confusion caused by millions of panic-stricken refugees on the roads.

The Russians face the problem of interdiction of lines of communications from allied air strikes or nuclear bombardment. The reliability of the East European forces and populations must also be in doubt. While they may not be faced with hordes of refugees moving eastwards, they must reckon with acts of sabotage or various forms of non-co-operation.

An assessment of the theatre nuclear balance is complicated by the difficulty of distinguishing between weapons systems belonging to the central strategic balance and those whose function lies exclusively within the regional theatre. The American Poseidon warheads are counted into the central balance under SALT, but some are allocated to

SACEUR. On the other hand, Russian central systems are not counted into the theatre balance, although some of them are probably targeted on Europe. With or without Poseidon, it is calculated that NATO is at present at a disadvantage *vis-à-vis* the Warsaw Pact in terms of *arriving warheads*, but that it can expect a substantial improvement in capability with the introduction of new long-range systems from 1983.[20]

The hazards and uncertainties of attempting to draw up a balance-sheet between the opposing forces do not alter the fact that any attack by one side or the other would in all likelihood escalate into a major conflict whose outcome would be so uncertain that any objective would be disproportionate to the risk. The prospect of such a war in Europe would not only be devastating for the Europeans but to the superpowers as well. One must therefore conclude that the basic conditions of mutual deterrence remain and will continue to remain in spite of some disturbing developments in recent years.

The other conclusion which forces itself on the observer is that the balance is only maintained by the continued involvement of the United States. Without American equipment, technology and nuclear weapons there would be no military balance at all unless the West European states embarked on a massive rearmament programme, which would be politically unacceptable.

The strategic balance in East Asia has a very different character from that in Europe. One is not dealing with the confrontation of two alliances but with a complex relationship among four major states: the two superpowers and two regional powers. Most of Russia's ground and air forces in the region are directed against China. The forces facing Japan are relatively small: one division in Kamchatka, two divisions in Sakhalin, one division (about 6,000 men) in the occupied northern territories. They are backed up by more than ten divisions in the maritime provinces, whose main target is China, but some of which could be used as reinforcements against Japan.

In terms of equipment, the Soviet forces are certainly equal and in a number of instances superior to Japan's SDF, but their main lines of communication are vulnerable and liable to be disrupted in a major conflict. For this reason and for wider strategic objectives, it is assumed that the main purpose of the Soviet military build-up in this area is defensive; to protect its position in the Sea of Okhotsk, its lines of communication in the Sea of Japan, and its access to the Pacific.

The novel feature in the region has been the steady expansion of Soviet naval, air and strategic nuclear forces, challenging the hitherto uncontested American superiority, if not domination, in these fields. The most noteworthy developments in recent years have been the strengthening of the Pacific Fleet with a *Kiev*-class aircraft carrier and other major surface vessels, including the first of the new *Ivan Rogov*-class amphibious assault transport/dock ships, and a great expansion of the number of submarines, especially those carrying ballistic missiles. The stationing of ten *Delta*-class SSBN in the Sea of Okhotsk, capable of hitting any part of the American mainland, has brought the region well into the central strategic equation.

Soviet nuclear strategic and air power has reached a new dimension with the introduction of the formidable SS-20 intermediate-range ballistic missile (IRBM) and the Backfire bomber, capable of reaching most of Asia. IRBM and shorter-range missiles have also been deployed on Sakhalin and Kamchatka. Once Backfire bombers armed with long-range anti-ship missiles are introduced into the Pacific Fleet, they will pose a very serious threat to the American navy and further undermine its protective role.

The Seventh Fleet is, however, a formidable fighting machine, backed by the even more powerful forces of the Third Fleet in the Eastern Pacific. In addition, the United States deploys some conventional forces in the region: one army division and one air-defence brigade in South Korea, one division and one air wing of the Marines in Japan, and some Marine Corps amphibious units elsewhere. They are supported by an extensive network of bases in the Western Pacific, and could be rapidly and substantially reinforced in a crisis. On the whole, the United States and associated powers retain the strategic advantage in East Asia, which is as much a function of Russia's geographical limitations as of anything else.

Continuity and Change in American Policy

Any assessment of the future direction of American policy must begin by making a distinction between declaratory and real policy. Beneath the high-flown rhetoric of every incoming administration, always promising to open a new chapter in American history and to fulfil some great American dream, there is a much greater continuity than meets the eye. Détente began to break down under Carter, and Mr Brzezinski's attitude towards the Soviet Union was not so different from that of his successors.

The breakdown of détente was not the result of any specific policy switch but of a whole series of events. They included changes in military technology and their impact on perceptions of the balance between East and West, the Iran hostage crisis and its impact on American public opinion — arousing very strong nationalist sentiment which turned against what was seen as a decade of decline and retreat; and the Soviet blundering into Afghanistan.

President Reagan struck a responsive chord in the American public with his determination to stand up to the Russians, to make America strong again,[21] and his emotional appeal to patriotism and ideological fervour.[22] By the time he had reached the half-way mark of his term in office, the President's policies displayed the hallmarks of pragmatism and confusion that are the distinctive features of the American style of policy-making.

Negotiations were underway on Strategic Arms Reduction Talks (START) in place of SALT. Negotiations over the control of Long-range Theatre Nuclear Forces (LRTNF) in Europe were resumed. The President had launched his 'zero option' initiative on arms control.[23] The controversial MX ICBM programme, inherited from the previous administration, was modified. The embargo on the export of grain to the Soviet Union had been lifted. Some of this was in response to economic constraints, other initiatives, especially over arms control, were attempts to calm public disquiet at home and abroad.

The militancy of public utterances about the Soviet threat hides a cautious approach to the superpower relationship in line with the ground-rules worked out over the decades. In spite of all the crisis talk, nothing much seemed to have changed. In the summer of 1982 Afghanistan had almost ceased to be an issue between East and West. Poland had taken its place and seemed set to go the same way.

Yet there are indications of some fundamental changes in the basic direction of American policy which call into question the security relationships among the Western allies. The upward and downward proliferation of nuclear weapons once again raises the issue of a decoupling of the central strategic balance from theatre balances. This has been the subject of an intensive debate over the past two or three years, and has accounted for the remarkable revival of the Campaign for Nuclear Disarmament (CND) in Britain and its even more remarkable spread to other West European states. It is bringing new life to the anti-nuclear sentiment of the Japanese people just when it had begun to show signs of decline, to the extent that some publicists had even dared to raise the question of a Japanese nuclear armament.[24]

The issue is not new and recalls earlier debates surrounding the deployment of tactical nuclear weapons on the continent of Europe. At that time the European allies feared simultaneously a localized nuclear conflict fought by the superpowers over their territories, and a weakening of the deterrent because of a presumed American reluctance to defend Europe for fear of a global holocaust.

The current debate originated with the decision of the Carter Administration to adopt changes in American strategy which had hitherto stressed the concept of MAD. The new strategy was counterforce in conception and covered Soviet Military targets, including hardened missile silos and command centres. The proposed modernization of Western theatre nuclear weapons and the introduction of the Soviet SS-20 heightened anxieties that both superpowers were now putting their emphasis on the ability to fight a limited nuclear war which could be confined to Europe.

Such fear may well be exaggerated. Once started, it seems improbable that a nuclear conflict could be controlled and contained so neatly. If the experts are right, the introduction of new TNF may have been merely a further reinforcement of deterrence:

> Any Soviet or American President, faced with the decision to 'go nuclear', must assume that to do so would mean losing control over events and probable mutual destruction. Consequently, the mutuality of risk in all-out nuclear war also makes limited nuclear war less, not more, probable.[25]

Nevertheless, the interest of nuclear strategists in limited nuclear war; the emphasis that governments on both sides place on their ability to fight such a war; the encouragement to take the possibility of such a war seriously, especially through so-called civil defence programmes; and the risk of accident or miscalculation on either side in a situation where each has first strike capabilities and thousands of weapons, are all reasons enough for people to be suspicious of the complacent optimism of the experts. In the final analysis effective deterrence rests on convincing the opponent not only of one's *ability* but also of one's *willingness* to use such weapons. And if deterrence should break down, what better than to have contingency plans which would limit the damage — that is, avoid devastation of one's own territory — while one seeks a compromise solution with the enemy?

The whole debate has brought to the fore the question whether the existing alliance structure, that gives the United States such a decisive role, still serves the interests of the European partners. The problem has not yet arisen in Japan, but might surface if there is a move to distinguish between TNF and central strategic forces in the Asian region —

a likely development in view of the deployment by the Soviet Union of ICBM as well as SS-20 and Backfire bombers.

In sum, deterrence remains the basic American idea, but it is a reversion to the traditional military concept of deterrence, which approximates more to the Soviet doctrine of nuclear strategy. The risk that a conflict arising from accidental or minor armed clashes will escalate rapidly into a nuclear war cannot be ignored. This would be particularly true at a time of acute international tension when both sides are geared to counterforce strategies.

Matters are worst for Europeans and Japanese, who might find themselves at the centre of a limited nuclear conflict before the machinery of signalling and consultation can put a stop to the escalator. Their perceptions, limited to the regional environment, are bound to be very different from those of the United States with its global view.

It is this difference that points to a potentially more far-reaching and fundamental change in American policy. That is the increasing attention to containing Soviet expansion in regions of the world which have hitherto escaped or been only marginally drawn into the East-West confrontation. This development is, of course, a consequence of the greatly extended reach of Soviet military power.

Europeans and Japanese are, therefore, urged to commit themselves to sharing the responsibilities and burdens of a global containment policy. First signs of this are the readiness of the British to assist in policing the Gulf through the development of a rapid-deployment capability — a reversal of the policy of withdrawal from East of Suez — and the Japanese undertaking to extend naval operations beyond the territorial waters and the 200-mile Exclusive Economic Zone (EEZ).

American pressures are behind the debate over changes in the structure and scope of both the Atlantic Alliance and the US-Japan Security Treaty system, in order to accommodate the requirements of global security. The terms of the North Atlantic Treaty would have to be amended to remove the geographical restrictions. This might be acceptable to the government of Mrs Thatcher, but to hardly any other member of the Alliance. The smaller members would reject it for obvious reasons. The Federal German Republic would be unwilling to enter into specific commitments because of its special security problems as well as political if not constitutional constraints. France might be willing for joint action on an *ad hoc* basis, and has already demonstrated this in Africa and by the despatch of naval units to the Indian Ocean, where it maintains more warships than either the United States or the Soviet Union. On the other hand, it would be no more ready to accept any arrangement whereby its military policy might be dictated by the actions of the United States, than it has been in Europe.

The conversion of the Atlantic Alliance into a global alliance by the inclusion of Japan, Australia, New Zealand, ASEAN and some of the Latin American states would raise still greater problems. Such a development would be generally unacceptable; Europeans and Japanese would see it as a diversion of resources from their own security needs. Not only might it require deployment of their own forces to remote regions at a time of crisis when they would also be needed at home, but it might encourage the Americans to reduce their commitments to Europe or Japan on the grounds that American forces were more urgently required elsewhere. This is what happened in 1979-80 when units of the Sixth Fleet in the Mediterranean and the Seventh Fleet in the Western Pacific were sent to the critical Gulf region. Under a unified alliance structure such a shifting of forces would be even more easily accomplished than at present, when the United States has to justify every move and reassure its partners in the separate alliances. Such reassurances might be more easily dispensed with in an all-embracing alliance in which the United States, through its special position and global spread, would decide what is best in the interests of all.

Creating the formal structures of a global alliance would present such inherent difficulties and would require an extraordinarily high degree of political will on the part of all the countries concerned that, short of extreme provocation by the Soviet Union, its establishment is not within the bounds of practical politics. Various forms of looser association appear to be more immediately practicable and are being aired in some quarters.

One such is the so-called trilateral system of Europe, North America and Japan, which is being approached from two directions. One has been via the annual summit meetings of the leading industrialized states (the US, Canada, France, Britain, the Federal Republic of Germany, Italy, Japan), the first of which was held at Rambouillet in 1975 in the wake of the oil crisis provoked by the Yom Kippur War. Their purpose was to coordinate the economic policies of the powers in the face of major changes in the world economic system. Their agendas have been dominated by trading and fiscal problems among themselves and by the problems of the so-called North-South Dialogue with the developing world, especially the resource-rich countries. A new tone appeared in these proceedings at the Venice Summit in June 1980, when the seven heads of government united in a condemnation of the Soviet invasion of Afghanistan. The significance of the occasion lay in Japan's association with the statement. The other six are accustomed to dealing with such matters within the context of the Atlantic Alliance.

The other path towards trilateralism has been through the establishment of the unofficial but influential Trilateral Commission in the early 1970s.[26] It provided a useful forum for the sharing of ideas about co-operation between the United States, Western Europe and Japan. Its main purpose was to exchange views and promote common positions in the economic and cultural fields. Underlying it, however, was a wider concept of shared interests. Trilateralism represents a particular view of the Western 'alliance' in which the United States is not only by far the most important member but also the hinge between two self-contained security systems.

The American interest in an expansion and eventual linking of the security systems which they have underwritten since the Second World War involves more than a mere pooling of Western military strength. It demands the coordination of the diplomatic, economic and ideological content in Western policies. However, in pursuing this objective the United States may find itself increasingly at odds with its partners. Although the crude indicators of Russian military might are such that Europeans and Japanese are bound to see it as a potential threat, it does not follow that they regard it as the most immediate or the most important threat.

For countries that are very dependent on the import of sources of energy and other essential raw materials, a greater and more urgent danger arises from the political and social instability of large regions of the world, and the tendency of the superpowers to see such disturbances primarily in terms of their rivalry. They have shown a marked predisposition to regard any civil war or interstate conflict in the Third World as a kind of zero-sum game between themselves.

The possibility of a superpower clash in the Third World, either directly or, as is more likely, through proxies, is only one and not the most important reason for alarm. There is no evidence that either the Soviet Union or the United States is any more willing to risk a direct confrontation in those parts of the world than in Europe and Northeast Asia. Russian inaction over the Israeli siege of Beirut in the summer of 1982 and the limited American response to the Soviet invasion of Afghanistan are indications of this caution.

The contest is fought by other means: propaganda, subversion, the supply of arms, financial and economic aid, and the mobilization of friends and allies. The effect of such methods often runs counter to the interests of the industrialized states. For example, American policies in the Middle East have hurt the economic and political interests of the other Western powers, whether in their relations with Iran or with the Arabs, and have prompted them to follow independent policies in the region, much to the annoyance of the United States.

Such differences go beyond perceptions of the Soviet Union and the pursuit of economic interest. They are symptomatic of an even wider problem. The superpowers act under a tacit agreement that they are the guardians of world order. It is an order built on their overwhelming might and the moderation of their mutual rivalry. But in practice neither is able to control its client states, so that their efforts to divide the world into neat spheres of influence are continually frustrated, not so much by the activities of the other superpower but by the unpredictable behaviour of those countries. Indeed, their interventions have the paradoxical effect of making the rest of the world even more restless and unruly, arousing nationalist or religious passions, and encouraging ambitious states to play off one superpower against the other.

The agenda of the security relationship between the industrialized states and the United States, therefore, includes the problem of world order, in addition to the problem of perceptions of the Soviet Union and the requirements of maintaining a military balance between East and West.

Notes

1. Vice-President George Bush, referring to the pipeline dispute when speaking in Chicago, 27 August 1982. *The Times*, 29 August 1982.

2. 'à moins d'événements qui, au cours des trois prochaines années, viendront à changer les données fondamentales des rapports entre l'Est et l'Ouest, elle [France] serait en 1969 [after which any party could leave the Alliance following a year's notice – Article 13] et plus tard, résolue, tout comme aujourd'hui, à combattre aux côtés de ses alliés' Letter from de Gaulle to President Johnson, 7 March 1966. Jouve, *Le Général de Gaulle et la construction de l'Europe*, Vol. II, pp. 544-5.

3. M. Margaret Ball, *NATO and the European Union Movement* (London, Stevens & Sons Ltd for the London Institute of World Affairs, 1959), pp. 88-9.

4. It seems ironic in view of contemporary European apprehensions about being dragged into a conflict against their will, that the element of Article 5 which emphasizes that an attack on one or several members should be considered as an attack on all, was inserted to meet European demands for an unambiguous commitment, whereas the phrase which gives some freedom of action to each member state was inserted to meet the American wish to have room for manoeuvre in any response to the outbreak of hostilities in Europe. See Général André Beaufre, *L'O.T.A.N. et l'Europe* (Paris, Calmann-Lévy, 1966), pp. 31-2.

5. Robert E. Osgood, *NATO – The Entangling Alliance* (Chicago, The University of Chicago Press, 1962), p. 253.
6. Kelleher, *Germany and the Politics of Nuclear Weapons*, p. 5.
7. Jouve, Vol. I, pp. 64-6, 719.
8. Martin E. Weinstein, *Japan's Postwar Defense Policy 1947-1968* (New York, Columbia University Press, 1971), pp. 96-7.
9. Osgood, pp. 331-2.
10. See Wolf Mendl, *Issues in Japan's China Policy* (London, Macmillan for the Royal Institute of International Affairs, 1978), pp. 7-16.
11. For Kissinger's description of the doctrine of linkage, see Henry Kissinger, *The White House Years* (London, Weidenfeld & Nicolson and Michael Joseph, 1979), pp. 127, 129-30.
12. *Japan* (London, Japan Information Centre, Embassy of Japan), No. 122, 12 November 1980.
13. *Strategic Survey 1978* (London, International Institute for Strategic Studies, 1979), p. 10.
14. L.W. Martin, *British Defence Policy: The Long Recessional* (London, Institute for Strategic Studies, Adelphi Paper no. 61, 1969).
15. For the text of what was formulated later as the 'Nixon Doctrine', see 'Informal Remarks in Guam with Newsmen, 25 July 1969' (*Public Papers of the Presidents of the United States: Richard Nixon 1969*, Washington, DC, United States Government Printing Office, 1971), pp. 548-9, 551-2; also Kissinger, *The White House Years*, pp. 222-5.
16. The methodology and difficulties involved in making comparisons are usefully discussed in *The Military Balance 1977-1978* (London, International Institute for Strategic Studies, 1977), pp. 102-10.
17. *Asian Security 1981* (Tokyo, Research Institute for Peace and Security, 1981), pp. 65, 75-7.
18. Among these is the failure of the armed services to attract and retain people of good educational background. The problem is compounded by the effect of the abolition of the draft in 1973, which has meant a reduction of ready reserves of people with recent military experience from a peak of 1.5 million in 1972 to 400,000 in 1979. There are also increasing problems over the serviceability and maintenance of sophisticated military equipment. Many weapons apparently fail in service through inadequate maintenance. *Strategic Survey 1979*, pp. 35-6; *The Military Balance 1980-1981*, pp. 4-5, *1981-1982*, p. 4.
19. For a discussion of some of the technical weaknesses of Russia's strategic forces, see *The Defense Monitor* (Washington, DC, Center for Defense Information), vol. IX no. 8, 1980, pp. 2, 4.
20. For a fuller discussion of the balance of theatre nuclear forces, see *The Military Balance 1981-1982*, pp. 126-9.
21. A Gallup poll conducted in September 1979 – before the election of President Reagan – indicated that 60% of the electorate favoured increased defence expenditure and only 9% were in favour of reductions. Eight years previously, an identical poll yielded 11% and 49% respectively. *Strategic Survey 1979*, p. 33.
22. See the text of President Reagan's Inaugural Address, 20 January 1981, *Guardian*, 21 January 1981.
23. In this proposal, made on 18 November 1981, President Reagan offered to cancel the planned deployment in Europe of Pershing II and ground-launched cruise missiles, if, in return, the Soviet Union would dismantle existing SS-4, SS-5 and SS-20 intermediate-range missiles.
24. This was dramatically illustrated by the conversion of one of the postwar intellectual leaders of the pacifist movement to the view that Japan should have its own nuclear weapons. Ikutarō Shimizu, 'The Nuclear Option: Japan Be a

State!' (*Japan Echo*, vol. VII no. 3, Autumn 1980, pp. 33-45, a shortened translation of 'Kaku no Sentaku: Nippon yo Kokka tare', *Shokun*, July 1980).

25. *Strategic Survey 1981-1982*, p. 1.

26. For a discussion of the concept of trilateralism and its place in American perceptions, see Robert Immerman, *European Attitudes Towards Japan: Trilateralism's Weakest Link* (Washington, DC, Department of State, Foreign Service Institute, April 1980), pp. 1-2.

4 RELATIONS WITH THE SOVIET UNION

Over the past thirty-seven years Japan and the major states of Western Europe have faced the same basic security problem: the containment of Soviet power. Allowing for regional variations, their relations with the Soviet Union have followed roughly parallel courses, falling into three chronological phases: the first covers the years immediately after the war until the mid-1950s; the second spans the next two decades; the third began in the mid-1970s.

The Early Postwar Years

In the 1940s and early 1950s, the threat from the Soviet Union was essentially a revolutionary one. Wherever a communist party flourished there was a danger of Soviet intervention by 'invitation'. Cominform had replaced the prewar Comintern as the unifying instrument of world communism under Russian control. The misery and confusion of the postwar years in Berlin, Japan, France and other Western countries presented the Soviet Union with opportunities to get its foot into the door. The Prague *coup* of 1948 was a frightening example of how a communist party could exploit the situation after it had acquired key positions in the coalition government of a liberal-democratic society.

In these early years the challenge was basically political. It is true that the Soviet Union had established its East European empire as a result of the advance of the Red Army in the last stages of the struggle against Nazi Germany. Between the end of the war and the summer of 1947 it had absorbed Poland, Romania, Bulgaria and Hungary. All except Poland had been enemy countries and were under Soviet occupation, and it was under this regime that the three stages of absorption were carried out: first, coalition government under Soviet supervision; then occupation by communists or their sympathizers of key ministerial posts, such as Interior and Justice; and finally communist takeover by a variety of methods, such as mass demonstrations, the forced merger of communist and socialist parties, the deposition of the monarch, and so on.

Military force in these situations served as a potential threat but not as an instrument to effect the changes. In two instances where the attempt to establish or confirm Soviet domination failed, it is noteworthy that the Red Army was not used to impose Russia's will, even though it had the power to do so. At the end of the war Finland was at the mercy of the Soviet Union. It was allowed only a very limited military establishment, and had to lease a base to the Russians.[1] However, the Finns were successful in keeping communists out of the government and prevented a communist takeover, in spite of being a defeated nation and a hostage of Soviet military power.

When Yugoslavia was expelled from the Cominform in 1948 and an anathema pronounced against Tito's regime, the Red Army did not occupy it, although in a good position to do so from bases in neighbouring countries. Tito's defiance of Stalin received some verbal encouragement from the West, but there was no formal commitment to come to his assistance. The main reason for the Soviet hesitation in using strong-arm methods to bring the Yugoslavs to heel was the remarkable unity of the country under Tito's leadership. In both Finland and Yugoslavia it was the health of the body politic which was the greatest obstacle to Soviet domination.

It was precisely the weakness and division of some of the Western states that offered the greatest opportunity for Soviet intervention through subservient communist parties. The danger was clearly spelled out in an article in *Pravda* of 12 January 1949:

> In our time one can be a sincere revolutionary and internationalist only by unconditionally supporting the CPSU and the Soviet Union itself, only by basing one's actions on the principles of Marxism-Leninism and proceeding from the experience of the Russian Communist Party — the leading force in the international Communist movement.[2]

With very strong communist parties in France and Italy, with Berlin surrounded by a communist-run Soviet Zone and the city's administration in danger of falling under communist control, and with the Japan Communist Party securing 10 per cent of the vote in January 1949 and the largest number of seats it has ever held in the Lower House of the Diet,[3] the Soviet threat was identified with subversion. It was recognized that the first line of defence had to be the economic and social recovery of the countries thus threatened, and this was the objective of the Marshall Plan and the turn-about in early 1948 of American occupation policy in Japan from punishment and reform to rehabilitation and reconstruction.

The shift of emphasis towards military confrontation occurred in Europe around the time of the Berlin Blockade (March 1948-May 1949) and in East Asia with the outbreak of the Korean War (June 1950). That is not to say that the West suddenly woke up to the existence of a Soviet military threat, or that the Russians suddenly decided that they would try to achieve their objectives with military means. The switch came about because of Western economic measures to stabilize the situation in Germany, in order to reduce the burden of the occupation, and to prevent the kind of chaos which would have played into the hands of the communist movement and prepare the way for the Russian domination of Germany. The communist campaign for reunificiation and the establishment of a People's Council in East Berlin in March 1948 would have provided them with a ready-made tool with which to take over the whole country.

The failure to work out a common economic policy with the Russians, principally because of differences over reparations, and the subsequent establishment of a unified regime in the three Western zones of occupation, cemented by the currency reform of February 1948, led to the final division of Germany and the first test of strength over Berlin. The Berlin Blockade has been aptly described as a Russian substitute for war, being an attack on the Western position in Germany and on the American commitment to Europe. Its failure led the Russians to abandon their attempt to 'conquer' Germany and to accept its permanent division. As a result, the Western powers and the emerging West German state, the draft of whose constitution was completed on the day the Russians lifted the blockade, had also assumed a commitment to West Berlin.[4]

The lines of confrontation in East Asia were drawn during 1949 and 1950, and the war in Korea set the final seal on a situation which was to remain frozen for the next two decades. Containment of communism in East Asia became part of a global policy of containment in 1949 after the communist victory in China and the signature of the Sino-Soviet Treaty of Friendship, Alliance and Mutual Assistance in February 1950. Japan had its place in the pattern of containment, but not apparently South Korea. Acheson's statement drawing the line of US positions to the east of the Straits of Tsushima[5] is only one piece of evidence of American ambivalence over Korea, for the United States was becoming disenchanted with Syngman Rhee and his regime.[6]

The North Korean invasion of the South was seen at the time as evidence of a readiness to use military force in the pursuit of communist expansion, masterminded from Moscow, in areas where American commitment was either absent or doubtful. Scholarly analysis since then[7] points to a much more complex situation in the communist camp. China, it seems, had been manipulated and out-manoeuvred by Stalin, and the bitterness and resentment caused by this were important factors in the eventual split between the two countries. Moreover, China's intervention in Korea may have been as much a measure designed to forestall a Soviet occupation of Manchuria, ostensibly for the defence of North Korea, as a reaction against the American advance towards the Yalu river.

Just as the appearance of a monolithic communist bloc was deceptive, so it is an over-simplification to think of the first postwar decade as wholly dominated by efforts to stem the advance of Soviet power in the two regions. The interaction of East and West was more complex than that. There were many in the Western countries, Churchill the most outstanding among them, who predicted an inevitable clash with Russia over Europe and elsewhere on the peripheries of the Soviet Empire. Some saw it as the operation of the 'natural law' of international relations: nature abhors a vacuum (Central Europe and a disintegrating China in this case), and there must be a power struggle to fill it. Others saw it as the advance of a militant ideology, and for them the struggle against the Axis powers had been a diversion, though a necessary one, from an ideological conflict which had begun before the rise of Fascism. A third group saw the Soviet 'threat' as a combination of the Russian obsession with security, great power behaviour, and a militant ideology.

There were, however, just as many who did not foresee an East-West conflict as a 'natural' phenomenon. Their main concern was to make sure that there would be no German revival, such as had followed the First World War, and they saw Russia as playing its part in the creation of a European system designed to make sure that this would not happen again. The first postwar security treaties in the West, the Treaty of Dunkirk between Britain and France (1947) and the Brussels Treaty (1948) between them and the Benelux countries, were sold to the public as reassurances against German aggression, though for many in government the real enemy was already the Soviet Union. The idea of working *with* Russia rather than *against* it was certainly foremost in French thinking in those early years. Ernest Bevin, who saw things less simply and was conscious of the dangers of Russian pressure, wanted Western Europe to develop a power that was equal to that of the United States and the Soviet Union, enabling it to become a 'Third

Force'.[8]

Such less stark prognoses of relations with the Soviet Union were strongly reinforced by popular perceptions that the communist 'threat' was either exaggerated or non-existent. The European public in the early years after the war was in a mood for radical change and left-wing policies. The Soviet Union had been a greatly admired ally, and its sufferings touched a chord of sympathy and fellow-feeling. Furthermore, the memory of the interwar years and the miseries of the depression had profoundly affected the generation which was taking over the leadership in Europe.

It is also far from certain that the Russians were bent on the conquest of Europe or even the satellization of Eastern Europe in the early postwar years. No doubt they were willing to benefit from the confusion and weakness of many countries and to support their friends in the local communist parties who were riding high at this time, chiefly because of their role in the resistance movements after 1941. But there is no evidence of a masterplan for conquest. On the contrary, it has been argued that the initial postwar policy of Stalin, which allowed free elections in Poland, Czechoslovakia and Hungary to the disadvantage of the communists, indicated a readiness to accept the existence of neighbours which enjoyed the kind of freedom that Finland has had.[9] The argument goes on to suggest that if only the United States had used its undoubted military superiority at the time to enter into serious negotiations with the Soviet Union, the course of postwar history might have been very different. Bertrand Russell used a similar kind of reasoning when he called upon the Americans to threaten the Russians with their atomic bomb after the Prague coup.[10]

So the Cold War began in Europe, not because people suddenly became aware of Soviet aggression, but because the United States failed to use its power to force the Soviet Union into a negotiated settlement. Instead, when the United States decided that there was a Soviet 'threat', it concentrated first on rearmament and shoring up the Western states before trying to force the Russians' hand in negotiations. The Soviet response was twofold: to accelerate their own rearmament and to consolidate their grip on Eastern Europe.

The developments in East Asia were different, but here again the Americans missed an opportunity in China where their policy failed to exploit the contradiction between Soviet and Chinese interests, and they made no response to signals from the Chinese communists. The subsequent confrontation seemed as stark as the one in Europe, although ideological rigidities on both sides obscured the nuances and shifts of one's opponents. The Cold War postures hid Sino-Soviet tensions from American eyes, and made America's allies appear to be more united in the common cause than they really were.

The Era of Détente

The first historical phase ended with the consolidation of the Cold War structures, which included the confrontation between blocs in Europe across a divided Germany and the construction of the American containment belt in East Asia, stretching from Hokkaido to the Philippines, reinforced by the ANZUS Pact in the south and British positions in Malaya and Singapore. The differences between the United States and its most important friends in the two regions were subordinated to the overriding concern for security against the communist world.

The second postwar phase was distinguished by the attempt to set up ground rules for the management of the rivalry between the superpowers. This was a function of the emerging military equilibrium between them but also of the increasing complexity of the situation within each camp. The paradoxical effect of the efforts of the United States to stabilize and control the military balance was to lessen European and Japanese perceptions of a security threat, which the United States was exploiting in order to hold the alliances together and keep them in order.

The 'Open Skies' proposals of the Eisenhower administration, the Partial Test-Ban Treaty, the Non-Proliferation Treaty, European negotiations for mutual and balanced force reductions, the Helsinki accords, were all part of the attempt to institutionalize the unique superpower relationship. The structure of international relations in East Asia did not permit the kind of comprehensive multilateral negotiations that were launched in Europe, but the normalization of Japanese-Soviet relations in 1956, the Geneva conferences on Indochina, the series of diplomatic encounters between the Chinese and Americans in Geneva and Warsaw, followed by the opening of relations in 1971, as well as the spasmodic contacts between North and South Korea, all formed part of the general tendency to seek a relaxation of tensions. The various developments in Asia did not always affect the superpowers directly, but they would not have been possible without the emerging détente between them.

In Europe it was possible to revert to a more traditional pattern of set-piece negotiations within a formal framework of multilateral conferences. In Asia the rigidities of Cold War confrontation gradually lessened, providing more diplomatic options, not only for the superpowers but also for the regional powers. As a consequence, the relatively unambiguous dividing lines were replaced by an intricate web of conflict and co-operation among the four major states. This was most clearly demonstrated in the Korean Peninsula.

China and the Soviet Union were committed to the North, the United States and Japan to the South. But China and Russia also competed for influence over the North and, more recently, have been competing in the search for a relationship with the South, but in such a way so as not to antagonize the North. Japan and the United States were not in direct competition over the South, though their perspectives were rather different.[11] As a consequence of their *rapprochement* with China, they favoured increased Chinese influence in the North, but there was a risk in pushing this line of policy too far and thereby increasing the temptation of the South to seek a relationship with the Soviet Union. The competition and mutual suspicions of the four external powers created a strong presumption in favour of stabilizing the *status quo* in the hope of achieving a 'German solution' in the peninsula. For this, however, neither Korean government was ready.

The institutionalizing of the superpower relationship in this second postwar period, which could be observed elsewhere in the world, as, for example, in the Middle East, was not accomplished without occasional crises and interruptions. The Cuban missile crisis of 1962 was the most dangerous confrontation since the Berlin Blockade. The anomalous status of Berlin, which was regulated but not settled by the series of agreements at the end of 1971, remained a very sensitive barometer of East-West relations as well as a source of tensions. In East Asia, a series of crises over the Strait of Taiwan in 1955 and 1958 and the Vietnam war of the next decade prolonged the atmosphere of Cold War. The impact of the conflict in Indochina on superpower relationships was, however, remarkably slight. Instead, it raised difficulties among allies. It was a factor in Sino-Soviet antagonism and it created friction between the United States and some of its friends. Perhaps its most significant effect was on world public opinion, particularly in the United States.

The lessening of hostility between the Soviet Union and the United States and the scope for more independent policies among the lesser powers that it provided, opened the way for the independent stance of de Gaulle, the formulation of an Ostpolitik by the German Federal Republic, and the development of Japan's China policy, in which the element of competition with the United States was not wholly absent. Each of the four Western states in our study began to develop a distinctive policy towards the Soviet Union, which the United States did not always disapprove of, and sometimes even encouraged.

Under de Gaulle, France wanted to make Russia a partner in the management of Europe, which for the French was still essentially the 'German Problem'. De Gaulle's successors had a less grandiose vision, but they were prepared to work *with* and not only *against* the Soviet Union. In its opening towards the east, a policy which folowed the unsuccessful attempt to isolate East Germany through application of the Hallstein Doctrine,[12] the Federal Republic of Germany abandoned its claim to sole legitimacy for the more subtle position of accepting two German states in one nation. The successive agreements with the Soviet Union, East Germany, Poland and other East European states, strengthened its position as the fulcrum on which any European settlement had to turn. The British, in keeping with their commercial reputation, chose the role of middleman, successfully over the test-ban negotiations, less so over Vietnam. In Asia, Japan sought to steer a course between China and the Soviet Union, trying to use its relations with the one as a lever in negotiations with the other.

The more independent policies of the European states and Japan, which reflected their increased self-confidence, were accompanied by a generally more relaxed attitude towards Russia. Problems of domestic order were decoupled from the Soviet 'threat'. This change was brought about by growing prosperity in the West, by the fragmentation of the communist monolith with ideological friction, and the rise of 'national' communism within the Soviet bloc and, in the 1970s, among the communist parties of the Western countries.

The revolutionary wave of the late 1960s which hit both Western Europe and Japan, was not linked to a Soviet threat. No government, apart from the French, was seriously shaken by the narrowly based movement led by intellectuals and students. Even in France the powerful communist party and the communist-controlled trade union federation rallied to the defence of the establishment. Moreover, the revolutionaries had a distinctly anti-Soviet orientation and sought their inspiration from elsewhere.

The Rise of International Tensions

Some aspects of the deteriorating international climate, which marked the closing years of the previous decade and the beginning of the 1980s, have already been touched upon in Chapter 3 (see especially pp. 64-8) and need not detain us here. However, there is an insufficiently understood correlation between the heightened international tensions and the impact of the deepening economic depression on the industrialized societies.

Economic factors undoubtedly influenced the course of electoral politics, bringing to power conservative governments in Britain and the United States, committed to very hard-line policies towards the Soviet Union. Similarly, after a decade of decline, the ruling Liberal-Democratic Party of Japan saw a reversal of its fortunes in the elections of 1980, and there has been a notable increase in the strength of its right-wing elements. In the Federal Republic of Germany the SPD/FDP (Social Democrat/Free Democrat) Coalition continued its precarious existence until it broke up in September 1982 and was succeeded by a CDU/CSU/FDP coalition. Although the socialist victory in the French elections of 1981 seemed to contradict these tendencies, there was a slackening in its reformist drive a year later and some evidence of a revival of conservative forces. All these domestic developments were accompanied by a greater emphasis on security and defence – a not unwelcome diversion from pressing and distressing economic problems.

Whether the deepening economic crisis and heightened tensions in East-West relations are really connected or not, the perception of a rough strategic equivalence between the two superpowers certainly increased apprehensions about the Soviet Union. Because of the harsher international climate, the old double fear of the Europeans, which first surfaced in the 1950s and was then subdued in the benign atmosphere of détente, is now more acutely felt than ever before.

On the one side is the fear that nuclear weapons are being integrated into war-fighting strategies, and that in the process of conducting a limited (for them) nuclear war, the Soviet Union and the United States will be prepared to lay Europe waste before they reach a settlement. The other fear is exactly the opposite. The United States may not, after all, want to risk escalation to intercontinental exchanges, and will therefore be prepared to settle with the Soviet Union at the expense of European interests. Western Europe might thus be gradually 'Finlandized'.

The first fear has revived the campaign for nuclear disarmament on a European scale. The second fear has spurred some governments to greater defence efforts, and to put more emphasis on the need to strengthen the alliance with the United States. The NATO commitment to an annual increase of 3 per cent in defence expenditure in real terms was intended to demonstrate to the Americans that the allies are making sacrifices for the common cause, and to signal to the Soviet Union that the alliance is very much in business.

Both fears may turn out to be hallucinations. The danger that limited exchanges would escalate to all-out nuclear war is such that neither side would want to risk any confrontation which might involve the use even of the smallest nuclear weapon. So, after all, it is possible that we may look forward to another thirty years of military stability in Europe!

The fear of 'Finlandization'[13] rests on a false appreciation and a false analogy which deserves a little digression. It is really quite insulting to the Finns to stigmatize their postwar relations with the Soviet Union with an ugly word, and to insist that this is what the West Europeans must avoid at all costs. The Japanese have acquired a similar perception, and it was alleged that when Foreign Minister Sonoda reported to his colleagues that Mr Kosygin had suggested to him that Soviet-Finnish relations should serve as a model for improved relations between Japan and Russia, the Cabinet was rendered 'speechless with impotent rage'.[14]

Finland has been remarkably successful in its foreign policy.[15] In spite of the fact that it was an enemy country during the war and at the mercy of Soviet power afterwards, it avoided occupation by the Red Army, succeeded in persuading the Russians to withdraw from the naval base of Porkkala in 1955, which eight years previously had been leased to the Soviet Union for fifty years, and, above all, it preserved its liberal-democratic institutions and free market economy, in spite of the existence of a pro-Moscow communist party and some difficult passages in relations with the Soviet Union. There has, of course, been a price which had to be paid in the form of Finnish neutrality and in a certain restraint on anti-Soviet criticism. None the less, Finnish neutrality is a far cry from Finnish 'satellization'.

Finland's position is unique in its corner of north-eastern Europe, with the Soviet Union to the east and south, neutral Sweden to the west, and NATO Norway to the north. Its geopolitical situation has undoubtedly influenced Soviet behaviour, but the main reason for the success in retaining its national integrity and in resisting pressures to draw it deeper into the Soviet orbit[16] has been its political stability and the great skill of the two statesmen, Paasikivi and Kekkonen, who dominated its postwar history up to 1980.

The Finns have one advantage over many of the Soviet Union's neighbours. By keeping their social and political system intact they have given the Russians no excuse to intervene in 'defence of socialism', as they did in Czechoslovakia in 1968 and as they might do in Poland. They did come perilously close to this kind of intervention on the outbreak of the 'Winter War' in 1939, when they set up a 'Democratic People's Government' of Finland under the communist leader Otto Kuusinen. There is, however, all the difference between the attempt to establish and impose a puppet government from outside and a move to establish, support, or restore such a regime from within a country.

Operating from a relatively secure domestic base, Paasikivi and Kekkonen shrewdly conducted their country's foreign policy. Both cultivated personal relationships of confidence and trust with the Soviet leadership. They were sensitive to Russian security interests, avoiding any formal identification with the US. They tried to strengthen Finland's independence with balancing relationships and various initiatives. They developed links with the Nordic group of states and thus indirectly with NATO — there is a kind of symmetry between Finland's security relationship with Russia and Norway's relationship with the United States. Finland was the first European state to recognize the two German governments, and it has assiduously promoted commerce with EEC and the European Free Trade Association (EFTA), with which it has a much larger volume of trade than with the Council for Mutual Economic Assistance (COMECON).[17] Another buttress of Finland's position was the policy of internationalization: taking initiatives at the UN, sending units for peace-keeping operations in Cyprus and the Middle East, acting as host to the first European Conference on Security and Co-operation and to the Strategic Arms Limitation Talks.

To imply that 'Finlandization' would mean slavish subservience to the Soviet Union is to over-simplify Finland's position. To go on to suggest that this could be the fate of Western Europe is to ignore essential differences between the two entities. It is unlikely that a state would enter into an analogous relationship with the Soviet Union unless it was in a fairly isolated position bordering on Russia. Austria's neutrality, which is much more along the classic lines of the Swiss or Swedish models, has a different character because it was born out of the four-power occupation and because Austria lies exactly between the two blocs. To talk of the 'Finlandization' of West Germany, France, Britain or Japan is hardly realistic when one takes into account how deeply embedded these countries are in the Western camp. Moreover, supposing the Americans do withdraw from Western Europe or Japan, the size and strength of the countries concerned would be such as to present the Soviet Union with a very different problem from that posed by Finland. This would be particularly true if an American withdrawal from Europe was accompanied by substantial progress in West European political unity, for which the apparatus is already in place.

If, however, a pro-Soviet communist party or a pro-Soviet left-wing coalition came to power in any one of these countries, then a move towards the Soviet camp might follow. Or, alternatively, the Soviets might be invited to intervene in an incipient or actual civil war. In such situations, a country could slide into a satellite status.

The fears about the Soviet Union that have re-emerged at the beginning of the 1980s bear some superficial resemblance to the fears of the Cold War era, and the reactions, both among the nuclear disarmers and the 'let's arm to the teeth' lobby, may be similar to earlier reactions, but the problems of threat and security have assumed different dimensions.

The essential difference from the Cold War period is the decline in American global dominance and the corresponding increase in the Soviet global presence. There is no longer a world order underwritten by American military might and economic domination. European and Japanese global interests are, however, almost exclusively economic, and the Soviet Union poses only one potential threat to them. Others come from the economic power of resource-rich countries, from political and social instability, and from the behaviour of the United States, as in Iran.

A new element has, therefore, entered the dialogue over security in Europe and East Asia. The Americans are inclined to make discussions about security against Soviet military power conditional upon agreement over the threat of Soviet power in the world at large, whether it be in the Middle East, Southern Africa or Central America. Given the ambiguous nature of threats to European and Japanese interests elsewhere, there is an understandable reluctance among those countries to see security in such simple terms.

The second major difference from the earlier postwar period is that the Soviet Union no longer poses such an obvious domestic threat. The fragmentation of the international communist movement has meant that often only small communist parties retain their unquestioned allegiance to Moscow. Even where a large party has apparently remained Stalinist and pro-Moscow, as in France, the appeal of the party to its traditional power-base in the electorate has been effectively challenged.[18] Other parties, such as the Italian party, have become almost hostile to the Soviet Union, which is in a dilemma over how to handle the phenomenon of Euro-communism.[19]

If the threat of slavishly obedient communist parties and potential fifth columns has receded, a new menace faces the industrialized societies: mass unemployment. This phenomenon, which many thought had been banished for ever by the Welfare State and government management of supply and demand, has now returned not merely as the effect of a cyclical recession experienced under a free-market system, but as the symptom of a much more disturbing restructuring of the economy, often referred to as the technological revolution. This is a process to be measured in decades, and the success of governments will be assessed on how smoothly and humanely they handle the transition. In the meanwhile the social cohesion of these societies will be sorely tried, and the emergence of extremist groups of the left and right poses a new threat to their stability. The ability of the Soviet Union to exploit these weaknesses is uncertain. Being itself a very conservative society, new-style revolutionary movements may appear to be just as threatening to the Soviet rulers as to the liberal democracies, as witness their tacit support for de Gaulle in his troubles in 1968, or their implacable hostility to Trotskyism.

Finally, the security problem that faces West Europe and Japan at the start of the 1980s is further complicated by the intricate economic relationships that have sprung up between them and the Soviet bloc. In the 1940s and 1950s Europe and Japan were busy with economic revival, and for this they relied very largely on the United States. Interdependence with the Soviet Union has been the fruit of détente, and it was an important influence on West European and Japanese reactions to the Soviet invasion of Afghanistan. It is, therefore, to the Soviet political and economic system and the delicate balance of mutual interests and mutual antagonisms between Russia and the industrialized states that we must turn next.

The Paradox of Soviet Power

Only one feature of the Soviet Union's place in the world today is universally accepted: Russia has become 'visible' everywhere and its 'interests' extend to every corner of the globe. But that is where the agreement ends. The significance attached to the presence of Soviet warships and merchantmen in every ocean, to Soviet military and technical assistance in many Third World countries, to the availability of naval and other military facilities and the presence of Soviet, Cuban and

Relations with the Soviet Union

East European military personnel in various parts of the world, and to the strategic implications of all this, are subject to various and contradictory interpretations.

Leaving on one side the Soviet apologia for this spread across the world — every imperialist power cloaks its expansion in some higher purpose, even if it is only resistance to a rival imperialism — there are two basic theories which seek to explain the rise of Soviet power. One sees it as a deliberate act of policy in pursuit of a grand strategic objective: the envelopment, isolation and ultimate destruction of the Western World, and the eventual triumph of a socialist world order under Russian domination. The other accepts that this may be the declared objective of the ideologues of Soviet communism, though obviously not put as crudely as that, but maintains that it has little direct bearing on Soviet policy, which is opportunistic, seizing what advantages it can with as little risk as possible, and concerned as much with security against external threats as with expansion. Indeed, territorial expansion, especially on the perimeters of the Soviet Union, is an ambiguous phenomenon; it can serve both defensive and offensive purposes.

The 'drive for world domination' theory relates to the conspiracy theory of world events in which the external threat is part of the internal subversive threat, all master-minded from Moscow. The advantage of this approach is that it is simple and comprehensive. If you believe in it, then everything falls into place. Industrial disputes, race riots, spy scandals, nuclear disarmament campaigns, Cubans in Ethiopia and Angola, Russian fishing fleets in the South Pacific, guerrillas in El Salvador, are all exploited in the service of the overriding objective. One weakness of the simple and comprehensive theory is that the facts do not fit it. The world communist movement is fragmented and bitterly divided against itself and can no longer be manipulated at will from one centre. Another weakness is that it attributes a much greater constancy of purpose and ability of execution to the Soviet government than actually exist. There may be very broad objectives behind Soviet policy, such as the enhancement of Russia's security, power and influence in the world, and the promotion of the communist cause, but they are so general and vague as to be no more than slogans based on some philosophical principles and of little use as guides to practical policy.

This, on the whole, is the argument of those who prefer to lay stress on the element of opportunism in Soviet policy. They maintain that the Russians do not operate in a vacuum, that they are influenced as much by domestic and external factors as any other power, and that far from creating and shaping events, they constantly react to the international environment and events beyond their control. By and large, the prevailing view among the leaders of the West has inclined towards this position, but they have differed in their assessment of the dangers inherent in Russian opportunism.

Some, including Henry Kissinger,[20] see it as a particularly ruthless kind of opportunism. They point to the doctrinal underpinnings of Soviet policy, which expands 'The arena of international struggle ... to include the internal policies and social structures of countries, mocking the traditional standard of international law that condemns interference in a country's domestic affairs.[21] They also stress the dangers stemming from the closed and very secretive policy-making system of a totalitarian society. As Kissinger puts it: 'The Soviet leadership is burdened by no self-doubt or liberal guilt. It has no effective opposition questioning the morality of its actions'.[22]

Kissinger is rather cavalier in his treatment of history when he accuses the Russians of 'mocking the traditional standard of international law' by interfering in the domestic affairs of other countries. The record of the past two centuries raises the question whether great powers have done anything else but 'mock' this 'traditional standard'. The revolutionary governments of late eighteenth-century France set the example in this respect and the members of the Holy Alliance, led by Kissinger's hero Metternich, were not beyond meddling in the affairs of other states when the established order appeared to be threatened. The allied powers at the close of the First World War did the same when they intervened in Russia from all sides in an attempt to destroy the Bolsheviks. Kissinger's own account of American activities in Chile[23] provides another example of intervention in the domestic affairs of a sovereign state.

The advantages enjoyed by totalitarian regimes in the field of foreign policy cannot be denied. Once the Politburo has decided on a particular line of action, it is comparatively easy to carry out and justify in the absence of public debate or of electoral calculations. The unwieldiness and inefficiency of a highly centralized state apparatus in executing policy is, however, often overlooked by those who are impressed by the advantages of a totalitarian over a liberal-democratic system. Since discipline in the one-party state is ensured largely by human inertia and fear, the machinery of state is neither very flexible nor a source of imaginative and creative enterprise. Ruthless opportunism may convey an impression of greater determination and less caution than the Soviet state actually displays. Russian reluctance to intervene in Poland after the start of the crisis in August 1980 indicated both caution and hesitation.

European and Japanese perceptions tend to incline to the latter interpretation of opportunism. Their own traditions as great powers of the past encourage them to offer a more mundane and cynical explanation of Soviet behaviour, which might be less obvious to Americans with their traditionally optimistic and idealistic view of international politics. According to the European and Japanese view, the Soviet Union has to be seen as it really is: an imperialist power whose expansion depends as much on domestic constraints as on anything else.

Those constraints include an economy that is stagnant, with an agricultural sector unable to meet the requirements of the country, so that the government has to rely on annual imports of grain from the United States. The civilian and consumer industries are deprived because of the diversion of huge resources to military and prestige industries, such as the space programme. The highly centralized state apparatus and the dead hand of a huge and inefficient bureaucracy stifle initiative and enterprise. The whole is underpinned by a police system which tries to suppress any departure from state orthodoxy in word or deed.

In addition to these general features, there are several specific problems which have shorter or longer-term effects on policies and are of particular concern to the neighbours of the Soviet Union. One of these is energy; another the ability to control the East European glacis — a problem closely linked to the supply of energy. A third problem, pointing to the end of the century, is posed by the changing demographic structure of the Soviet Union.

Like the West, the Soviet Union is facing an energy crisis, but it is of a very different nature from that of the rest of the world. There is no decline of reserves, only a problem of getting them out of the ground and transporting the sources of energy to the regions where they are most needed. In that sense, there is no dependence on other countries. The Russians have, in fact, benefited from the rise in the price of oil over the past decade, which has had such a baleful influence on the economies of the Western World. Price rises have meant greatly increased earnings for the Soviet Union. In another sense, however, they are dependent on the Western industrialized countries, including the United States, for the capital and technology to exploit their vast resources of natural gas, coal, and oil.

Russia's energy crisis has, therefore, an altogether different appearance. The annual rate of economic growth has declined steadily since 1974, and for the first time sank below 3 per cent in 1980. The production of crude oil, which accounts for 45 per cent of all sources of energy, is slowing down. The Eleventh Five-year Plan set the same target for the production of oil in 1985 (600 million-645 million tons) as was set for 1980 by the Tenth Five-year Plan, and it is extremely doubtful whether the target will be reached this time. On the other hand, the Soviet Union will find it very difficult, if not impossible, to reduce its exports of sources of energy to Eastern Europe because of the dangerous consequences of doing so, both in increasing hardship and causing social unrest, and because it would drive the East Europeans to look elsewhere for their supplies with all that would mean in weakening the Russian hold over those countries. It would be equally unpalatable to reduce exports to the West European countries because energy provides two thirds of Russia's badly needed hard currency earnings.[24] Here, rather than in some masterplan for world domination, lies the explanation for the Soviet interest in the energy resources of the Middle Eastern region. The Soviet Union is already importing natural gas from Afghanistan and Iran in order to be able to export its own resources to Eastern and Western Europe.

Any weakening of the infrastructure which links the economies of Eastern Europe to that of the Soviet Union and is reinforced by their dependence on Russian sources of energy, would be seen by the Russians as highly dangerous. The prospect that some of the countries would be drawn into the Western orbit is probably exaggerated; the prospect that, given half the chance, they would move into some sort of neutral or non-aligned posture, is much more likely. It would revive the prewar pattern of a string of weak, unreliable, and potentially hostile states on the borders of the Soviet Union. Above all, however, any change in the international status or the domestic political structures of these countries would be regarded as a challenge to the legitimacy and credibility of the Soviet Union; the legitimacy of its role as 'protector', guide and philosopher, and the credibility of its control over the region. The periodic popular eruptions in all these countries, except Bulgaria, over the past three decades are proof of the fragility of the Soviet dominion over the East European states. The feeling among the masses, with the exception of the minority who benefit from the Russian presence and influence, is profoundly anti-Russian.

A longer-term problem concerns the changing character of the population of the Soviet Union. This is a complex matter and not confined to the fact that on present demographic trends the Great Russian element in the total population will have become a minority by the turn of the century. While the rate of growth among the European populations is declining, that of the Asian populations is increasing. It is, therefore, likely that more attention will have to be paid to the needs and aspirations of these peoples, and that an increasing number of non-Europeans will begin to occupy command positions in society. The process may not be an easy one as there is a strong racialist undertone in Russian attitudes which the official ideology has not expunged.

The orientation of the state, which has been predominantly towards Europe, apart from brief moments in its history, may gradually turn towards the south and east. Such a tendency will not only reflect a shifting ethnic balance in the Soviet Union, but the fact that two-thirds of Soviet territory lies east of the Urals and contains most of the Soviet Union's actual or potential energy resources, minerals, precious metals and timber.

The great stirrings in the Islamic world cannot fail to affect the Soviet Union's muslim population. Other groups, Koreans, Mongols and Chinese, also have their kinsmen across the border. Russia has been quite successful in keeping its non-European populations reasonably quiet and contented in the past, but its ability to continue doing so will depend on the government's skill and the impact of external events. The chief points of friction will be the problem of the extent and degree of the continued 'russification' of these populations, and the determination with which the authorities will insist on ideological rectitude. A harsh and unbending policy in both spheres may provoke serious unrest and provide opportunities for centrifugal influences.

Ethnic and demographic shifts also have an economic dimension. For the first time in its history, European Russia is experiencing a shortage of labour, so that the non-European population of European Russia may increase substantially in the future. The armed forces may also acquire more and more of a non-European complexion. But the growth points in the economy are in Asian Russia, and here there is a shortage of skilled labour. Instead of bringing the sources of energy and raw materials to industrial centres over great distances and at enormous costs, Soviet economic planning is turning towards the creation of major industrial centres near the raw materials. The development of Eastern Siberia and the maritime provinces into a giant industrial complex may take place in the more distant future, and might be launched once the second Siberian railway (BAM) is completed around 1985. Industrial development around the oil fields of Western Siberia and near the Urals is already well under way.

Such changes will be difficult and expensive to execute. Geography and an inhospitable climate are major obstacles, and it will require substantial incentives to persuade people to settle in those regions. None the less, the traditional pattern of a European Russia, which contains the country's major industrial centres, and a vast underdeveloped Asian hinterland, is changing; a change which will be facilitated by the rise of the Pacific region as the world's most important economic area.

Mutual Interests and Mutual Threats

The relations between the Soviet Union and its European and Japanese neighbours are a compound of mutual interests and mutual-threat perceptions.

The mutual interest is fashioned by the prospect of economic co-operation. The prospect is more immediate and based on surer ground as far as Western Europe is concerned. It is much less clear and rests on shakier foundations for Japan. The Soviet search for economic co-operation with Western Europe dates from before the first oil crisis of 1973-4. Its objectives were both economic and strategic: the satisfaction of the need for access to high technology and the loosening of ties between Western Europe and the United States.

Although progress towards achievement of the second objective was not very noticeable in the 1970s, differences between West European and American attitudes towards relations with the Soviet Union sharpened with the growth of tensions between the superpowers at the beginning of the 1980s and, more indirectly, as a result of the depression which grips the world economy. Europeans and Americans have always had different conceptions of the connection between economic co-operation and détente. The Americans have tended to see economic co-operation as a concession for détente and the good behaviour of the Soviet Union, a view related to the doctrine of linkage as spelled out by Henry Kissinger. For the Europeans, economic co-operation was the consequence of détente.[25] They have entered into it as a long-term commitment, as in the twenty-five-year agreement between the Federal Republic of Germany and the Soviet Union, signed in May 1978.

The Americans have preferred short-term agreements, subject to renegotiation at regular intervals. It has been said that it would be easier to use such agreements, rather than a long-term exchange between investment and the supply of energy, as instruments of pressure or punishment. This is not altogether convincing, as President Reagan found out. Far from intimidating the Russians with the ban on the export of grain, he was forced to relax the restrictions under pressure from his own farming lobby. Moreover, the Soviet Union could and did turn to alternative markets in Argentina and elsewhere;

so much so, that in 1983 it refused to buy extra supplies from the United States, though urged to do so by a hard-pressed American government.

Co-operation over the exploitation and supply of sources of energy is the crucial feature of economic relations between East and West in Europe. Not that there has been no substantial trade in other areas, but the importance of energy derives from its strategic significance and the binding nature of such agreements. Thus, within five years, from 1973 to 1978, the supply of Western capital goods for the development of energy resources in the Soviet Union increased twelvefold.

The strategic importance of collaboration in this field is underlined by the known Soviet objective of an all-European energy conference to work out an understanding for long-term collaboration, independent of East-West relations and conflicts in other areas, and for a basic agreement over financing. The West Europeans, on the other hand, want co-operation over energy to include a code of conduct in the Middle East which would safeguard Western supplies against Soviet exploitation of the political and social turbulence in the region. They are also interested in practical matters such as the free flow of information about the industry, agreements on management procedures, and so on.

Substantial supplies of natural gas are already being fed into the West European grid from the Soviet Union.[26] West European and Japanese firms are providing steel tubes and compressors for the 4,300-km pipeline scheduled for completion in the mid-1980s and due to transport up to 40 billion (UK) cubic yards (30 billion cubic metres) of natural gas from the Yamburg fields in Western Siberia to several European countries.[27]

In the summer of 1982 this became the subject of bitter controversy between West Europe and Japan on one side and the United States on the other. In pursuit of his policy of sanctions, President Reagan not only prohibited American firms from participating in the project, but also European and Japanese companies from using American technology, acquired under licence, in supplying equipment for the pipeline. All four states were involved, and accused the American Administration of extending its authority beyond its territory, of violating both international and American law, and of 'unacceptable interference in the independent commercial policy of the European Community'. The European Community also pointed out that the flow of Siberian gas at the maximum planned rate by 1990 would account for only 4 per cent of the Community's total energy consumption.[28]

Other proposals are in hand for the transmission of electricity to the

West European grid, and the Soviets are planning to increase the nuclear source of primary energy production from the current 2 per cent to 8-10 per cent in the year 2000; all this to be achieved with the help of capital and technology from the Western countries. There are also plans for the joint development of new technologies, such as the liquefaction and gasification of coal.

The prospects for Soviet-Japanese economic co-operation are no less discussed and there is no lack of projects and plans, but they involve a longer-term perspective and much greater uncertainties. The significance of such collaboration would only become apparent once the industrialization of Siberia and Soviet East Asia got under way. The region has great potential value as a source of energy (especially coal and natural gas), of industrial raw materials and, eventually, as a market for consumer goods. In addition, there are rich fishing grounds around the Kuriles and in the Seas of Japan and Okhotsk.

The Japanese do not want to be left out of the long-term development of the region, but their experience of economic relations with the Soviet Union has not been happy, having been fraught with uncertainties, such as when the Soviets rather abruptly suggested a cut in the amount of oil to be supplied to Japan from the Tyumen field, in whose development the Japanese were seriously interested, from a maximum annual target of 40 million tons to 25 million tons.[29]

A number of joint projects survived the sanctions policy after the Soviet occupation of Afghanistan, such as the exploration for oil and gas in the continental shelf off Sakhalin and the development of coal in Southern Yakutia. Others were suspended, such as the third stage of the development of lumber resources in Khabarovsk, or shelved. In spite of a relaxation of the embargo policy introduced in early 1980, the progress of Japan's trade and other economic relations with the Soviet Union remains sluggish, and has been outpaced by the economic relationship with China.

After a long period, during which they tried to steer a middle course between the Soviet Union and China, the Japanese began to show a clear preference for China, especially at the time of the signing of the Treaty of Peace and Friendship in August 1978, and they have energetically pushed the economic relationship ever since, in spite of many disappointments and setbacks. Whenever the business community was reluctant to risk further substantial investment, the government encouraged and supported it with cheap loans and other facilities.

The fundamental issue for Japan is where to put its money: in the prospects for a successful modernization of China or the prospects of the industrialization of Soviet Asia? The rivalry of the two powers makes the choice all the more difficult and hazardous. An example of the dilemmas facing Japan over its economic relationships with the two communist giants, even before the signature of the Sino-Japanese treaty, was the abandonment of plans to assist in the construction of the second trans-Siberian railway because of its potential strategic threat to China.[30]

For the present, at least, Japan shows most interest in the Chinese experiment, but it keeps its options open as much as possible, and this is indicated by the existence of joint projects with the Soviet Union and the continued discussions about others which are favoured by important economic pressure groups, especially the hard-pressed steel industry.

For Europe and Japan alike, the economic relationship with the Soviet Union cannot be separated from considerations of national security, either because of the complications it creates in relations with other countries (the United States in the case of Europe, China and the United States in the case of Japan) or because of their own fears of Soviet intentions.

The principal objectives of Soviet security policy are to acquire sufficient military strength to deter and, if necessary, defeat any would-be attacker. Related to this is a tendency to extend the defensive perimeter as far outwards as possible. The objective of increasing the Soviet presence and influence elsewhere in the world has a lower priority, and serves the purpose of forcing the United States on to the defensive, of distracting its attention and dispersing its forces.

The question which most concerns the states of Western Europe and Japan is to what extent the Soviet Union aims to include them in its defensive perimeter. Are the Russians serious when they insist that their military dispositions in both regions are strictly defensive, or is this a camouflage for preparations for an eventual onslaught aiming to overrun these countries and absorb them in the Soviet Empire? The problem is made more difficult by the fact that Soviet strategic doctrine follows the classic argument that military strength and offensive capability are the best instruments of deterrence and defence.

The practical implications of Russian security policy, whatever its ultimate intentions might be, have not only led to the build-up of a formidable and threatening military machine in Europe and to an analogous process in East Asia, but have encouraged the Western powers to adopt a similar approach in so far as their nuclear forces are concerned. For both sides, therefore, the hazards of remaining inactive in an acute crisis have become so great that there must be a strong temptation to strike first; each party fearing that it might be the victim of a pre-emptive attack from the other.

Nevertheless, a deliberate Soviet attack on either West Europe or Japan is the least likely of the Soviet options and is not taken seriously by the West, though obviously military planners do take it into account. It would be contrary to Soviet behaviour, and would take place only under the imminent threat of a war which seemed unavoidable.

Although Soviet efforts to extend the defensive perimeter will appear to the West as an attempt to gain control of Europe and Japan, the Russians are unlikely to add to the number of their satellite states unless the domestic circumstances of a particular country are such that it would fall into their lap without risk of a serious confrontation with the West. In spite of the great outcry over its occupation of a 'non-aligned' country in December 1979, the domestic conditions for Soviet intervention in Afghanistan had already been established in April 1978, and the Russians were probably surprised by world reaction because it seemed so obvious to them that Afghanistan had become nothing more than a 'protectorate' on the East European model.

Waiting for the opportunity to establish a direct influence over a state is essentially a 'passive' policy. The attempt to detach countries from association with the United States and to foster contradictions among the members of the Western Alliance is an 'active' policy, constantly pursued. Russian hostility to EEC is an instructive example. One should have thought that the emergence of EEC was to be welcomed as a factor which would increase the contradictions between Western Europe and the United States, but this is obviously outweighed by the fear of a strong West European bloc with a common foreign policy, exercising a great attraction over the East European satellites. The Russians prefer to deal with the Germans, French and British separately, and to exploit the differences among them.

The Soviet model for a 'satisfactory' relationship with the countries of Western Europe and Japan is probably the Agreement of Friendship, Co-operation and Mutual Assistance signed with Finland in April 1948,[31] especially the contents of Article 1 (Finland promises to fight and repel an armed attack aimed at itself or through its territory at the Soviet Union. Finland will operate within its territory, if necessary with the assistance of or jointly with the Soviet Union. Soviet assistance to be subject to mutual agreement); Article 2 ('The High Contracting Parties shall confer with each other if it is established that the threat of an armed attack as described in Article 1 is present.'); Article 4

(Neither party will enter into an alliance or coalition directed against the other); and Article 6 (The parties will respect each other's sovereignty and not interfere in each other's domestic affairs).

A treaty or agreement based on these terms would clearly imply the neutralization of the country; a severing of formal ties with the United States — even the most innocent commercial or cultural relations might be construed by a suspicious Soviet Union as a ganging up against itself; and the right of the Soviet Union to bring pressure to bear under the pretext of a perceived threat to itself or its partner. This, in fact, has been the experience of Finland, but, as noted earlier (pp. 93-4), the Finns have been quite successful in averting Soviet interference, and have even defied the Russians on several occasions without damaging consequences. The Russians, no doubt, would regard such arrangements as both necessary and legitimate measures for their security. None the less, Europeans and Japanese could hardly fail to see them as a first step towards absorption in the Soviet bloc.

The objective of loosening the structures and ties of the various alliances with the United States, leading first to a kind of neutralization and perhaps eventually to a closer association with the Soviet Union, has been secondary to the immediate concern for the consolidation of the gains made at the end of the Second World War and for stability on Russia's western and eastern flanks. For this purpose, the Russians have been willing to accept a continued American presence in Europe and the American protectorate over Western Europe in exchange for recognition of their protectorate over Eastern Europe. This arrangement has had the additional advantage of containing the German problem. In East Asia there have been some indications that while the Soviet Union is fearful of the formation of an American-Sino-Japanese 'axis', it might be willing to accept a continued American presence in and around Japan, if only as a means of preventing an even more feared Sino-Japanese alliance.

The formal division of Europe into three identifiable political categories: the Atlantic Alliance, the Warsaw Pact, and the neutral/non-aligned countries, was achieved in the 1970s with the series of agreements on Germany and Berlin and with the Helsinki accords. No political settlement is ever 'final', and there are sufficient loose ends and loopholes in these agreements to provide opportunities for further pressures and manipulation from both sides, as witness the continuing ambiguities of the situation in Berlin, the political importance of the human rights issue, and the difficulties experienced by the Russians of keeping order in their own sphere.

Although it is not only the West that has reason to be fearful, the Russians will undoubtedly want to make use of any opportunity to further their long-term objective. They will exploit domestic divisions within the Western countries, encouraging pacifist and neutralist tendencies, and make the most play of differences within the Alliance, especially over nuclear armament and energy policies. In Europe they give indirect support to campaigns for nuclear disarmament, in Japan they encourage Japanese-Soviet friendship associations, especially in Hokkaido, and reward those who are well disposed to the Soviet Union with fishing rights and other privileges.

The success of such movements in any one country may eventually lead to a policy of neutralism as the Finns interpret it. But the Russians are likely to push further, with the aid of veiled threats or blackmail, inviting auto-censorship and a policy of neutrality, such as the Russians interpret it.

The armoury to support this kind of Soviet pressure consists of diplomacy, political manipulation, propaganda of various kinds, economic and cultural measures. The weight of Soviet military power not only serves to defend the Soviet sphere, but also to create a sense of insecurity in the countries bordering it, which heightens the contradiction between those who want to deal with the 'threat' through increased armaments and those who are looking for a way out of the interminable arms race.

Whatever the outcome of the debate in the West, it seems that the Soviet Union could not fail to benefit. Increased armament creates political unrest by diverting resources from social welfare and raising fears of war; the shift towards neutralism would weaken American influence. But then, the Russians are hoist on their own petard. An arms race has the same nefarious impact on the Soviet economy, and there always remains the question of how much longer the long-suffering Russian people can be persuaded to accept the austere conditions of life which are imposed on them. On the other hand, a tendency towards the relaxation of tensions would increase the restiveness of the peoples of Eastern Europe who are also attracted towards neutralism and non-alignment.

Shared Interests in Different Environments

Europeans and Japanese share a fundamental interest: to convince the Russians that the United States has a stake in their security. On the other hand, they want their relations with the Soviet Union, especially in the economic sphere, to be undisturbed by tensions between the two superpowers and free from an American veto.

On the surface these appear to be incompatible interests. In reality, however, they illustrate the supreme paradox of the relationship between the superpowers. To be linked to one of them guarantees security against the other, but once this link is firmly established it offers a freedom of manoeuvre which derives from the security afforded by the superpower system. The opposing superpower dare not take offensive action for fear of a direct confrontation with the protecting superpower; and the protector dare not pull in the reins too tightly for fear of losing its protégé and thus weakening its own position *vis-à-vis* the adversary.

The shared interests of Europeans and Japanese have different practical implications which stem from their regional environments. The main concern of the West Europeans is with the impact of arms-control agreements between the United States and Russia on their own security — to resist any decoupling of the American deterrent from deterrence in Europe, and to avoid the supreme nightmare of a limited nuclear war in Europe. They are also deeply worried over the course of relations between the Soviet Union and its East European allies. The more precarious the Soviet control over those countries, the greater the likelihood that the Russians would pursue a hardline policy against the West. This would be particularly true if they felt their position in East Germany was being undermined.

A third preoccupation of the West Europeans is with the coordination of their foreign policies. Side by side with the existence of independent and competing policies, of which the approaches to the Soviet Union in the spring of 1980 by Giscard d'Estaing and Helmut Schmidt is a recent example, there is the search for the formulation of a European foreign policy. Its beginnings can be seen in the initiative of the Common Market countries over the Palestine issue, a certain coordination over the response to the hostage crisis in the autumn of 1979 and early months of 1980, with which Japan was associated, and the refusal to accept the American interpretation of events in El Salvador. However, it seems easier to work out common positions over extra-European problems than over those nearer home. In European matters the tradition of independent national policies is still too strong. Lord Carrington's visit to Moscow on 6 July 1981 to present the EEC proposals on Afghanistan, was a tactful exercise in warning the Russians against military intervention in Poland and could be said to have marked the start of a West European policy on East-West relations in Europe. American anxieties and actions over the projected pipeline may have had the effect of reinforcing this trend.

Such problems of coordination with regional allies do not concern Japan. The only states in East Asia which might be considered as potential allies are the Republic of Korea and the members of ASEAN. The long-term future and stability · of Korea are too unpredictable and mutual suspicions and animosities too great for there to be much likelihood of an alliance between Japan and its nearest continental neighbour. Moreover, constitutional constraints and domestic political inhibitions would seem to rule out any formal Japanese commitment. A similar set of reasons, plus the additional factor of geographical distance, would militate against a Japanese alliance with ASEAN. Moreover, the disparity between the economic strength and international importance of Japan and the economic and political weaknesses of the other states would make such alliances very unequal partnerships, in contrast to Western Europe where the leading states are of more-or-less comparable strength and status.

Japan is, and is likely to remain, an isolated actor within the context of a triangular relationship between the two superpowers and China. This is again in contrast to the situation in Europe with its bipolar structure. In spite of a trend towards bipolar alliance confrontation in the region (The Soviet Union/Mongolia/Vietnam *v*. China/Japan/United States/ASEAN), the criss-cross of interests suggests a much more confused pattern of relationships at several levels: the superpower level, the regional power level (China and Japan), and the subregional power level (a Vietnam-dominated Indochina, ASEAN, Korea), with potentially important powers on the fringes (Australia and India). Through its security treaty with the United States, its strategic position in Northeast Asia, its economic interests and influence, Japan is involved in international politics at all these levels simultaneously.

In spite of an accelerated movement towards the building up of its military strength, Japan will continue to be inhibited from using the military instrument in support of its foreign policy.

In terms of size, natural resources, population and nuclear armament it is not in the same class as the United States, the Soviet Union and China. It relies on the United States for its security against the Soviet Union to a greater extent even than the Europeans, but it does not share the European anxiety of becoming the main battlefield in a war whose course it cannot control. This is partly because of its geographical position and partly because North-east Asia is an area of secondary strategic importance for the two superpowers.

Thus, while the broad objectives of Western Europe and Japan may be the same: making sure of the American commitment without becoming dependent on the United States for the conduct of relations with the Soviet Union, the coordination of their policies faces formidable obstacles. The official position of all countries, though perhaps least in France, is that such co-operation can only take place within an association of states led by the United States. Nevertheless, there have been significant stirrings in recent years, and an increasing number of instances when Western Europe and Japan have shared similar if not identical positions over relations with the United States and the Soviet Union; and such developments are reinforced by their parallel interests in the problems of the Third World.

Notes

1. Articles 4, 13, 15, 17 and 18 of the Treaty of Peace between Finland and the Allied and Associated Powers, signed in Paris, 10 February 1947. Anatole G. Mazour, *Finland between East and West* ((Princeton, NJ, D. van Nostrand Co. Inc., 1956), pp. 261, 263-4, 272-3.

2. Quoted by Geoffrey Stern, 'The Foreign Policy of the Soviet Union', in F.S. Northedge (ed.), *The Foreign Policies of the Powers* (London, Faber & Faber, 1968), p. 88.

3. The JCP obtained nearly 3 million votes, and their membership in the House of Representatives rose from five to thirty-five.

4. Philip Windsor, *City on Leave: A History of Berlin 1945-1962* (London, Chatto & Windus, 1963), pp. 98-130.

5. 'This defensive perimeter runs along the Aleutians to Japan and then goes to the Ryukyus . . . The defensive perimeter runs from the Ryukyus to the Philippine Islands.' Remarks of Secretary Acheson before the National Press Club, Washington, 12 January 1950. (*The Department of State Bulletin*, vol. XXII no. 551, 23 January 1950, pp. 115-18).

6. Mineo Nakajima, 'The Sino-Soviet Confrontation: Its Roots in the International Background of the Korean War' (*The Australian Journal of Chinese Affairs*, no. 1, January 1979, pp. 19-47).

7. Ibid., *passim*.

8. He developed this idea in a Cabinet Paper in January 1948. Margaret Gowing, *Independence and Deterrence*, Vol. I, p. 242.

9. Henry Kissinger, *The White House Years* (London, Weidenfeld & Nicolson and Michael Joseph, 1979), p. 63.

10. When I was an undergraduate, I heard him advocate this position with his customary crystalline logic in an address to the Cambridge University Labour Club.

11. See Franklin B. Weinstein and Fuji Kamiya, (eds), *The Security of Korea: U.S. and Japanese Perspectives on the 1980s* (Boulder, Colorado, Westview Press, 1980).

12. Named after the State Secretary of the Federal Ministry of Foreign Affairs, who devised a policy whereby West Germany refused to maintain diplo-

matic relations with any government that had recognized the German Democratic Republic.

13. The term first came into use in the late 1950s or early 1960s. See, for example, Richard Loewenthal, 'After Cuba, Berlin?' (*Encounter*, vol. XIX no. 6, December 1962, pp. 48-55). Although Loewenthal never actually used the expression and did not even mention Finland in his article, it could be said that it spelled out the implications of the term.

14. *Guardian*, 28 July 1977.

15. Finland presents a fascinating case study of how a small state manages relations with the Soviet Union. To gain a balanced picture it is necessary to go to several sources for information. Max Jakobson, *Finnish Neutrality: A Study of Finnish Foreign Policy since the Second World War* (London, Hugh Evelyn, 1968) is an apologia for Finnish policy by one who helped to shape it. John P. Vloyantes, *Silk Glove Hegemony: Finnish-Soviet Relations 1944-1974: A Case Study of the Theory of the Soft Sphere of Influence* (Kent, Ohio, Kent State University Press, 1975) is an academic work which supports the thesis of 'Finlandization'. George Maude, *The Finnish Dilemma: Neutrality in the Shadow of Power* (London, Oxford University Press for RIIA, 1976) is perhaps the most balanced assessment of the three.

16. One such attempt was the 'Note Crisis' of 1961, when Khrushchev tried unsuccessfully to invoke the consultation clause of the 1948 Treaty of Friendship, Co-operation and Mutual Assistance. For the terms of the Treaty see Mazour, Appendix XII, pp. 280-2.

17. Fred Singleton, 'The Myth of 'Finlandisation' ' (*International Affairs*, vol. 57 no. 2, Spring 1981), p. 283, note 31.

18. In the French Presidential election of May 1981, the Communist Party candidate scored 15% of the vote, the lowest percentage ever obtained since the war.

19. See 'Eurocommunism 1978' (*Problems of Communism*, vol. XXVII No. 4, July-August 1978). Special issue with articles on France, Spain, and the view from Moscow.

20. Kissinger described Soviet policy 'as essentially one of ruthless opportunism'. (*The White House Years*, p. 119).

21. Ibid., pp. 117-18.

22. Ibid., p. 116.

23. Ibid., pp. 653-83.

24. Friedemann Müller, 'Das Energieproblem der Sowjetunion' (*Europa Archiv*, 36. Jahr, no. 3, 10 Februar 1981, pp. 87-96).

25. Müller, 'Das Energieproblem der Sowjetunion', pp. 90-1.

26. *BP Statistical Review of World Energy 1981* (London, The British Petroleum Company), p. 15.

27. As for Japanese involvement in the project, it was announced on 3 June 1981 that the Export-Import Bank would provide credits to enable Japanese steel-makers to export large diameter steel tubes and compressors for the construction of the pipeline. This, incidentally, was a response to pressure from business circles, alarmed that their European competitors were capturing orders with the assistance of export credits from their governments (*Japan Times Weekly*, 6 June 1981).

28. See text of document submitted by the EEC to the US government on 12 August 1982: 'Siberian Pipeline: Note of the Ten to the U.S. Government' (*Europe Documents*, Europe: Agence Internationale d'Information pour la Presse, Luxembourg-Bruxelles, no. 1216, 12 August 1982). Also, the report of a meeting between Ambassador Yoshio Okawara and US Deputy Secretary of State Walter Stoessel on 18 June 1982, *Japan* (London, Embassy of Japan Information

Centre), no. 199, 5 August 1982.

29. Mendl, *Issues in Japan's China Policy*, p. 102, note 5.

30. Ibid., pp. 74-5. The problem was, of course, more complicated than that and involved financial and economic considerations on both sides. For a more detailed discussion of the various aspects of Japanese-Soviet relations see Kazuyuki Kinbara, 'The Economic Dimension of Soviet Policy' and Wolf Mendl, 'The Soviet Union and Japan', in G. Segal (ed.), *The Soviet Union in East Asia* (London, Heinemann for the Royal Institute of International Affairs, 1983).

31. Mazour, pp. 280-2.

5 EUROPE, JAPAN AND THE THIRD WORLD

Any discussion of European and Japanese strategic policies in the world at large must focus on their economic interests. Apart from small pieces of British and French real estate scattered around the globe, mostly in the form of islands, the physical presence of the great powers of the past is confined to the merchants, managers and technicians engaged in many economic enterprises, and others who serve as teachers, advisers and voluntary workers in a variety of fields.

It is often argued that alongside the remains of an older form of imperialism, which include French domination of a number of their former African colonies from behind the scenes, and the presence of Western military and naval forces in a few independent countries, the economic influence and, in some cases, control exercised by the giant, multinational corporations of the industrialized countries, is merely a continuation of the old imperialism in a new dress. The accusation of a lingering imperialism may to some extent be justified, especially when one looks at the activities of France in Zaire, Chad and the Central African Republic in recent years. On the other hand, these can equally be regarded as isolated incidents, the exceptions that prove the rule, and no more than temporary holding operations, as illustrated by the course of events in Chad, where France has been caught between its residual obligations as a former imperial power and its economic interest in good relations with Libya.

The lesson of Suez (1956) is still valid today: military force is unreliable and, more often than not, self-defeating as an instrument for the protection of even the most 'vital' interests. At best it can be a delaying factor, as in Indochina (1946-54), Algeria (1954-62), and Aden (1964-7), or a means with which to buy time for a reasonable settlement of the tangled imperial legacy, as may turn out to be the case with the Falkland Islands. Within an international framework of the global competition between the superpowers, the rise of new regional powers in all parts of the world, a revolutionary ferment which knows no national boundaries, and the shifting balance of economic power to resource-rich countries in the Third World, the West European states and Japan can further their interests only through careful steering and manipulation.

What is more, the design and partial construction of factories and

Europe, Japan and the Third World 115

plants by Western enterprises in Third World countries, such as the joint Japanese/Iranian venture in building a petrochemical complex at Bandar-Khomeini, creates functional linkages which both sides will want to preserve at all costs for as long as the plant is under construction; the external technical assistance is irreplaceable, and the complex is valued by the host. In such cases military power is both useless and irrelevant in furthering Western interests. Even if the host country should scrap the project for one reason or another, it is very doubtful whether the injured party could gain redress through military action, which would not re-establish the partnership and only add to the overall loss in terms of cost.

In this chapter I propose to take a closer look at the relations of the four states with the Third World, in order to establish whether they form a sufficient basis for the emergence of a common policy towards it and the superpowers.

A Mosaic of Economic Interests

The interests of Britain, France, West Germany and Japan may be examined under several headings: the degree of their energy dependence on the Third World, their dependence on those regions for the import of other industrial raw materials, dependence on food imports, the character of their investment policies overseas, and the structure of their trade with the Third World.

The degree of their dependence on imports for primary sources of energy at the start of the 1980s is illustrated in Table 5.1. Japan is almost 100 per cent dependent on imports for its oil consumption. Germany and France are in a similar position. In 1980 Europe, taken as a whole, accounted for only 3 per cent of the world's oil production, while its share of world consumption was about 25 per cent. When it comes to coal, widely tipped as the major possible energy source in the next century and which is widely distributed outside the Middle East, it is significant that Japan tripled its dependence on coal within the decade 1965-76, and in this respect too is overwhelmingly dependent on imports. The European states, on the other hand, are relatively rich in coal resources, with the exception of France, and together import only about 16 per cent of their coal consumption.

The geographical origin of the imported sources of energy (Table 5.2) reveals that in 1979 both Japan and the European states were heavily dependent on the Middle Eastern region for oil, but Japan far

Table 5.1: Production, Import and Export of Primary Energy (expressed in common units of petajoules, except for Japan)

Energy source	Federal Republic of Germany Production	Imports	Exports	France Production	Imports	Exports	Production	UK Imports	Exports	Production	Japan Imports	Exports
Hard coal	2,586.0	264.8	355.8	622.8	687.5	14.8	2,994.2	66.6	59.4	18.027*	68,228	71
Crude petroleum	197.4	4,173.5	3.0	85.8	4,840.7	—	2,250.6	2,875.1	1,048.8	433*	217,186	—
Natural gas	613.8	1,367.6	83.9	307.1	643.8	6.4	1,390.4	182.6	—	99.4**	889.2	—
Nuclear, hydro and geo-thermal	586.8	—	—	959.8	—	—	419.1	—	—	13,240***	—	—

Notes: *Units in thousand tonnes
** Units in petajoules
***Units in thousand tonnes of coal equivalent

Source for European statistics: *Annual Bulletin of General Energy Statistics for Europe* (United Nations, 1982).
Sources for Japanese statistics: *1980 Yearbook of World Energy Statistics* (New York, United Nations, 1981); *Statistical Yearbook for Asia and the Pacific 1980* (Bangkok, Economic and Social Commission for Asia and the Pacific).

Table 5.2: Principal Sources for the Import of Hard Coal, Crude Petroleum and Natural Gas in 1979

Exporters	Federal Republic of Germany Coal	Federal Republic of Germany Crude petroleum	Federal Republic of Germany N. Gas	France Coal	France Crude petroleum	France N. Gas	UK Coal	UK Crude petroleum	UK N. Gas	UK Coal	Japan Crude petroleum	Japan N. Gas
Middle East	—	43,620	—	—	94,400	.7	—	40,720	—	—	183,590	65.6
Africa	1,050	43,130	—	8,430	22,470	119.4	70	4,680	25.0	2,410	630	—
N. America	2,280	—	—	3,440	—	—	1,030	—	—	24,080	—	55.2
Venezuela	—	1,360	—	—	820	—	—	1,740	—	—	450	—
Poland	2,220	—	—	4,460	—	—	650	—	—	550	—	—
USSR	210	3,580	352.6	740	5,000	94.3	60	2,020	—	2,340	7,380	—
W. Europe	1,430	15,270	1,072.4	7,640	4,170	477.3	250	3,940	323.6	330	—	—
Oceania	920	—	—	2,410	—	—	2,260	—	—	27,050	—	—
Far East (Brunei/ Indonesia)	—	430	—	—	500	—	—	—	—	—	48,060	611.4

Units: Coal: thousand tonnes
Crude petroleum: thousand tonnes
Natural gas: petajoules
Source: *1980 Yearbook of World Energy Statistics.*

more so than the others. It is true that Britain and France import most of their crude from the Middle East as well, though Britain could in an emergency do without such imports altogether. Both France and the Federal Republic also relied to a considerable extent on North African sources, and in the case of Germany the amount was almost equal to that derived from the Middle East.

Over 70 per cent of Japan's total oil imports pass through the Strait of Hormuz. Another major source of oil for Japan is Indonesia, and it is noteworthy that two other sources of energy, coal and natural gas, are obtained mainly from countries of the Pacific basin, such as Australia, the United States, Canada, Brunei and Indonesia. In contrast, Britain imports only small amounts of coal, mainly from Australia and North America. The two other West European states, France and the Federal German Republic, apart from deriving some of their coal and much of their natural gas from the Common Market area, rely to a striking degree on imports from the Soviet bloc. Japan, too, imports some of its coal from that source, especially Eastern Siberia.

When we look to the future, several trends may be discerned. European and Japanese expectations of energy dependence differ only in detail from each other, but differ substantially from those of North America. Japan is proposing to make the most substantial shift away from dependence on oil with the objective of reducing the share of oil in total energy supply to 49.1 per cent by 1990, as against 66.4 per cent in 1980.[1] It is intended to achieve this both through energy conservation and the development of alternative sources, as well as through economic restructuring, which implies a shift away from importing oil and other sources of *primary* energy to purchasing energy-intensive products which have been manufactured near the sources of energy in developing countries with the assistance of Japanese investment and joint projects. Direct dependence for sources of energy would thus be replaced by indirect dependence which, however, also implies certain strategic costs. Nevertheless, the most startling feature in Japan's expectation of reduced dependence on the import of petroleum has been the impact of conservation measures in relation to the growth of GNP, as illustrated in Figure 5.1.

A few years ago it was expected that with the depletion of oil and natural gas reserves in the North Sea, Western European coal imports would rise to 50 per cent of coal consumption by the year 2000. A similar pattern was forecast for natural gas. Since the current recession, the forecast for coal imports has been cut back, a trend reinforced by the reluctance of industry to convert from oil-fired to coal-fired steam-

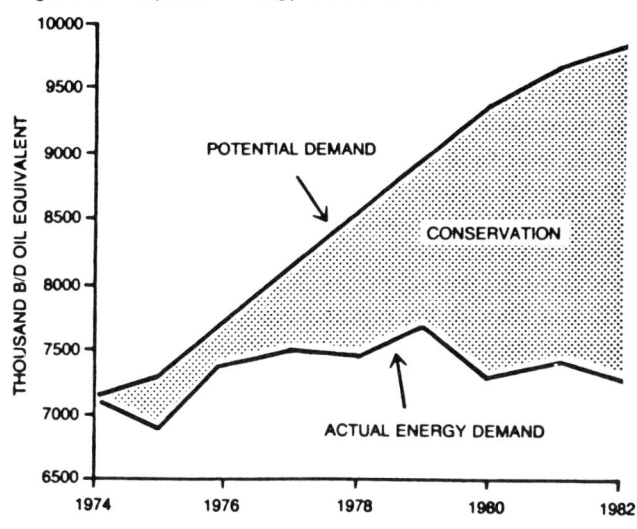

Figure 5.1: Japanese Energy Conservation

Source: Texaco Inc.

raising boilers. Both European and Japanese efforts to reduce dependence on imports by developing nuclear power do not really meet the problem. Technological and cost factors as well as strong domestic opposition raise very considerable doubts whether the pace of nuclear power-plant construction will meet the projections for nuclear-energy output, particularly in Japan. Furthermore, nuclear industry depends on the supply of natural uranium, which is found in relatively few areas of the world and might thus create a new kind of dependence syndrome.

In brief, by the turn of the century all four countries will still be dependent to a large extent on imported sources of energy, in which oil is expected to have an important share and the Middle East to be a major source of supply.

Analysis of recent trends in the demand for industrial raw materials reveals in each of the four states a high degree of import dependence in three key non-ferrous metals (Table 5.3). Aluminium is an apparent exception because of the level of domestic production of the metal. However, apart from France, the other states are very dependent on imported aluminium, especially bauxite ores. By 1981 the world recession had not greatly affected the percentage of domestic production of non-ferrous metals in relation to overall consumption and in a few

Table 5.3: Domestic Mine Production of Non-ferrous Metals as Percentage of Consumption, 1980/1

Metal	Federal Republic of Germany	France	UK	Japan
Aluminium*	70.1	71.9	91.5	66.7
	(71.3)**	(80.9)	(102.6)	(49.2)
Lead	9.4	13.6	0.7	11.4
	(8.7)	(9.1)	(0.9)	(12.3)
Copper	0.17	0.12	0.05	4.0
	(0.19)	(0.23)	(0.21)	(4.1)
Zinc	29.8	11.2	2.4	31.5
	(29.7)	(13.7)	(5.9)	(34.6)

Notes: *Only France has significant domestic bauxite for aluminium production, therefore 'production' refers to output from smelters, not mines as with other non-ferrous metals.
 **Percentages for 1981 in parentheses.
Source: Figures based on tables in *Metal Statistics: 1971-1981*, published by Metallgesellschaft AG

instances it had even been reduced. However, a continuing and deepening slump might have a substantial impact and considerably reduce the degree of import dependence.

The striking feature has been the growing Japanese and Federal Republic demand in the past. Until the 1960s Japan's consumption of metals formed a comparatively insignificant fraction of total world demand. By the beginning of the 1970s Japan was consuming a much greater share of world mineral production than its share of the GDP of the market economies.

The impact of the oil-price 'shocks', of the world recession, and of Japanese adjustments to these developments, lowered the growth rate by a half, but it was still very considerable in comparison to that of other industrialized countries. By 1980, therefore, its share of the consumption of world mineral production was more in proportion to its share of the market economies' GDP, which stood at 13¼ per cent in 1978. Germany's demand for industrial raw materials followed a similar line of development, though not so dramatically. Japan and the Federal Republic thus presented common features in contrast with the other two countries of the quartet.

The geographical origin of the industrial raw materials (Table 5.4) indicates significant regional variations. The sources of the three European states are generally more widely distributed than those of Japan.

Table 5.4: Principal Sources for the Import of Non-ferrous Metals and of Ores

	Federal Republic of Germany	%	France	%	UK	%	Japan	%
Bauxite	Australia	42	Guinea	72	Ghana	60	Australia	65
	Guinea	35	Greece	15	Greece	18	Indonesia	21
	Sierra Leone	13	Guyana	4	Sierra Leone	6	Malaysia	11
	Greece	3	Australia	3	France	5	China P.R.	1
	Guyana	3	China P.R.	2	Australia	4	Guyana	1
	China P.R.	2	Surinam	1	Surinam	3		
			Turkey	1				
Lead ores					[metal]			
	Canada	20	Irish Rep.	25	Australia	75	Canada	64
	Sweden	19	Morocco	19	Canada	19	Peru	17
	Morocco	11	Greenland	12	USA	4	Australia	10
	Irish Rep.	10	Rep. S. Afr.	12	Sweden	1	Rep. S. Afr.	4
	Thailand	8	Sweden	10			Thailand	3
	Peru	8	Australia	10			Rep. of Korea	1.5
	Rep. S. Afr.	8	Bolivia	4				
	Spain	5	Iran	3				
	Greenland	3	UK	2				
Copper (refined)	Chile	28	Belg./Lux.	28	Canada	28	Zambia	58
	Poland	20	Zambia	23	Chile	22	Chile	16
	Belg./Lux.	15	Chile	17	Zambia	15	Peru	11
	Zambia	10	Zaire	6	Belg./Lux.	7	Zaire	8
	Rep. S. Afr.	9	Spain	5	Peru	5	Canada	2
	Canada	5	Canada	4	Australia	4	Rep S. Afr.	2
	Zaire	4	Peru	3	Sweden	3	USA	1.5
	Australia	1	Australia	2	USA	3	Rep. of Korea	1.5
Zinc ores	Canada	36	Peru	26	Peru	31	Australia	34
	Sweden	12	Canada	19	Australia	28	Canada	32
	Greenland	10	Irish Rep.	15	Irish Rep.	19	Peru	24
	Irish Rep.	10	Sweden	12	Iran	8	N. Korea	6
	Peru	9	Bolivia	6	Canada	4	Philippines	2
	Rep. S. Afr.	8	Spain	4	Greece	4	Bolivia	1
	Mexico	7	Greece	4	Spain	3		
	Australia	3	USA	3	USA	1		

Source: Figures based on tables in *Metal Statistics: 1971-1978*, published by Metallgesellschaft AG

However, there is quite a heavy concentration on Africa, West Europe, North America (including Greenland), Latin America — especially for copper and zinc — and Australia, from which Britain imports a high proportion of its lead and zinc. Only the Federal Republic depends to any significant degree on a communist country, Poland, for one of the four non-ferrous metals.

If it can be said that the pattern of European dependence indicates a general concentration on the North Atlantic region and Africa, Japan's dependence on the Asia/Pacific basin is even more striking, with a particularly heavy concentration on relatively few countries: Australia, Canada and the states on the Pacific littoral of South America. Apart from bauxite, it imports only modest percentages of its requirements from East and South-east Asia.

In the last category of primary materials, food, Japan, the Federal Republic and Britain are much more dependent on imports than is France. However, it has to be remembered that the three West European states are part of the Common Market, which is self-sufficient in many essential foodstuffs and a net exporter of some. The agricultural sectors of the British, French and Federal Republic economies are directly affected by the Common Agricultural Policy. Taken individually, Britain and the Federal Republic are net importers of food, and Britain may have become more so in some respects as a result of its membership of the Common Market, whereas France is an exporter. For the purposes of comparisons it is, therefore, more meaningful to set Japan and the EEC side by side rather than the four states of this study.

In contrast to EEC, Japan's dependence on imports is expected to increase. By the end of the last decade it imported between 25 million and 26 million tons of grains annually, 17-18 per cent of the world trade in that commodity. In 1977 Japan depended on imports for 60 per cent of its total food requirements, that figure is expected to reach 70 per cent by 1990.[2] Even in those commodities in which Japan has been more-or-less self-sufficient, such as rice, vegetables, eggs and fish, there is expected to be a steady decline in self-sufficiency.

One important *caveat* must be attached to the foregoing discussion. Revolutionary developments in bio-technology may make a nonsense of traditional ways of looking at the food economy. Given energy, food can be manufactured as part of an industrial process, so that the question of import dependence becomes a question of energy supply. In view of Japan's position as a leader in the development of high technology, it could be that by the end of the century it will be more self-sufficient in food than the other industrialized states.

Official Development Assistance (ODA) and investment abroad are areas of national activity in which economic and politico-strategic interests meet. In terms of the total value of aid disbursed in 1980, the four countries were respectively second (France), third (German Federal Republic), fourth (Japan), and fifth (UK) after the United

Europe, Japan and the Third World

States in the league table of the members of the Development Assistance Committee (DAC) of the Organization for Economic Co-operation and Development (OECD). That was to be expected, given the size and importance of their economies. But in terms of the official development assistance ODA:GNP ratio, they occupy very different positions. In 1978, with a target of 0.7 per cent of GNP set by OECD, Sweden and Norway headed the list with 0.9 per cent and the Netherlands came next with 0.79. Of the major states, France had the highest rating (fifth) with 0.57. Britain was ninth (0.39), German Federal Republic tenth (0.31), and the United States and Japan shared eleventh place (0.23). Japan's ODA:GNP ratio rose to 0.32 per cent in 1980,[3] but its position in the league table has not improved.

If all forms of economic co-operation, including ODA, are added together, then the percentage of the total against GNP tells rather a different story. With a target of 1 per cent set by OECD, Switzerland headed the list with 4.24 per cent, followed by the UK with 3.27 per cent. Of the remaining major countries, France was fifth (1.68 per cent), Federal Republic of Germany tenth (1.13 per cent), Japan eleventh (1.09 per cent) — just above target, and the US thirteenth (0.73 per cent) — well below target.

The relatively poor showing of the major industrialized states, especially the richest among them (the US, Japan and West Germany), is an indication of the low priority given by such powers to international programmes from which they do not draw direct benefits in the form of increased strength and influence in the world. Moreover, in the case of Japan, this kind of action has not appealed greatly to the very ethnocentrically orientated Japanese.[4] The government's policy of doubling ODA at regular intervals has been a response to pressures from outside, and is designed to deflect mounting criticism from other Western countries of its relatively low defence effort.

The geographic distribution of aid further indicates the strategic importance attached to particular regions. The distribution of Japan's aid in 1980 was in the proportion of 70 per cent to Asia and 10 per cent each to the Middle East, Africa and Latin America. The principal beneficiaries in terms of value were Indonesia ($350 million), Bangladesh ($215 million), Thailand ($189 million), Burma ($152 million), and Egypt ($122 million).[5] The inclusion of Egypt among the top five is the result of Japan's policy of 'reinforcing' the West by channelling aid to countries of strategic importance, which occupy key positions in the front line against Soviet expansion. This, too, did not happen spontaneously, but initially as a result of pressures from its friends.

Hence, apart from the heavy emphasis on ASEAN, Japanese assistance has been given to countries such as Turkey, Pakistan, Egypt and Jamaica.

Similar patterns occur in the aid programmes of the West European states. Britain and France tend to follow the line of their old imperial associations — British aid is sharply focused on members of the Commonwealth; the French concentrate on Francophone Africa. The same applies to the superpowers, with United States aid predominant in Latin America, and the Russians assisting their clients in the Third World.

The picture that emerges from an analysis of the flow of investments is more varied. If anything it reveals a greater concentration on the pursuit of national as distinct from 'alliance' interests, however they are interpreted. Japan and France, and to a lesser extent the Federal Republic of Germany, have sought the security of essential supplies through the establishment of nationally owned extractive and processing industries or through joint ventures with the host governments. They hoped thereby to avoid excessive dependence on American and British-based oil and mining companies which, espcially in times of crisis, were seen as guaranteeing supplies to the metropolitan power at the expense of other customers.

Such a policy has, however, led to friction with the host governments and tended to force the companies into supporting uneconomic operations. As a consequence, there has been a move towards long-term purchase contracts covered by loans, a policy adopted by the Japanese and German metal-processing firms. The Japanese have often tied these loans to the export of Japanese equipment.

Another aspect of official policy has been the predilection for encouraging investment in 'safe' countries — allies or friends of the state, where there was less prospect that the *status quo* might be disturbed. One instrument for this is the provision of an officially sponsored insurance cover against 'non-commercial' risks. Both European and Japanese companies have been trying, so far unsuccessfully, to have this scheme extended to include 'unsafe' countries, and to remove the annual limit on the investments so covered.

A final point worth noting has been the underlying trend in Japanese investments towards a greater concentration in the industrialized countries and a slowing down of the rate of investment in the developing world. This reflects increased uncertainty over the course of events in the Third World; and in this respect the revolution in Iran, supposedly such a bastion of pro-Western stability, was a great shock. But it also reflects the use of investment as an instrument for market penetration, thereby creating problems in European-Japanese economic relations, which have a direct bearing on trade with the Third World.

Of all the major industrialized states, Japan is by far the most dependent on imports of sources of energy, industrial raw materials and food. This has led directly to its peculiar trade structure in which it has to sell manufactured goods in order to earn the currency with which to pay for its massive imports from resource-rich countries. As a result, Japan has run up huge balance of payments surpluses with North America and Western Europe and substantial deficits with a number of Third World countries, especially in the Middle East. It is this feature which has dominated the problem of economic relations in the non-communist world.

In other respects Japan does not appear to stand out from its partners in Europe. Its share of world exports in 1977 gave it third position after the United States and the Federal Republic of Germany, with France coming fourth and Britain fifth. As a gross exporter it may not be such a 'threat' as is commonly assumed, but from the point of view of other industrialized countries it is a 'threat' in the export markets for manufactured goods. This might be greatly sharpened should Japan enter the market in armaments, from which it was completely absent at the beginning of the 1980s. The government is under growing pressure from some sectors of industry to ease its ban on the export of weapons.

Japan's trade is also regionally based, with a heavy concentration on Asia and the Pacific. In the value of goods exported, four Asian countries (China, South Korea, Indonesia, Taiwan) topped the list of Japan's export markets in 1975. Similarly, four Asian countries (Indonesia, China, South Korea, Brunei) topped the list of sources of imports in that year.

One problem of assessing the relative weight of Japan and the three major European industrialized states and their impact on the world's economy, is whether to take the European states individually or as part of the Community. If, as would seem logical, we should take EEC as a whole, then its exports and imports far exceed those of Japan, and one gets a wholly new perspective on Japan's economic problem. It may feel as threatened by the competition from two giant entities, the United States and EEC, as they do by the flood of imports from Japan.

The perception of an economic 'threat' to Japan goes some way to explain its apparently aggressive economic policies. As leaders of the post-industrial revolution, the Japanese concentrate on high technology,[6] and have achieved unbroken success in areas they have chosen to master. In addition, having become a high labour-cost country, they have established assembly facilities in lower-cost countries of the Pacific basin through investment and the export of capital equipment within that region, thus extending their base for an ever more formidable onslaught on world markets. What the Japanese see as a bid for the survival of their crowded country, bereft of any significant natural resources other than the skill of its population, is seen from outside as a bid for world economic domination, based on a lead in high technology, the control of extractive and labour-intensive manufacturing industries in the Asia/Pacific region, and the penetration of other industrialized countries through exports and investment.

Competition or Co-operation?

Although Europe and Japan could be described as 'objective' allies' in many respects, and the preceding analysis has shown that they have much in common in their relations with the Third World, especially in their dependence on it for access to many primary materials, notably sources of energy, it is the friction in their bilateral economic relationship which has dominated their attitude towards each other. Are we, therefore, going to see ever more acute competition between Japan and the European countries in the 1980s, and will it spread to the Third World? Or is the Third World going to be an area of increased co-operation which will eventually reduce the difficulties in the bilateral relationship? The answers cannot be couched exclusively in economic terms, but also have to come from fundamental changes in mutual appreciation and understanding.

The Third World includes a number of newly industrialized countries (NICs) which, alongside countries such as China, the East European states and some of those in southern Europe (Spain, Portugal, Greece and Turkey), will play an increasing role in world development and influence the policies of the developed countries. South Korea, Taiwan, Singapore are all making inroads into the markets of developed countries, both at home and abroad, further undermining declining industries in the old industrialized world. A society such as Japan can cope with this because it is capable of remarkably efficient structural adaptation. Much of the new challenge from the NICs of Asia has been financed and equipped by Japanese enterprises, and Japan itself absorbs their products in exchange for the export of capital goods and technology.

At the other end of the spectrum of advanced countries is the United Kingdom, which has shown itself to be incapable of efficient restructuring since the end of the Second World War, and whose answer at present seems to be the resort to a crude form of monetarism as the instrument with which to effect the desired changes in the domestic structure and outlook, but on nineteenth-century principles of *laissez-faire*, in contrast to the skilful manipulation of the economy by the state in Japan or France.

Although France, and to a less marked degree, Germany, share in the general European preoccupation with Japanese competition, they are psychologically and structurally better equipped than Britain to respond and eventually surmount the current difficulties. The present danger is not that Japan will relapse into a xenophobic nationalism, but that some of the Euorpean states, especially Britain, will be tempted along that path.

The problem of restructuring also has a direct bearing on whether the relationships between Europe and Japan in the Third World will be competitive or co-operative. If we take the model of economic progress to be expansion on the lines pursued hitherto, with an increasing demand for scarce sources of energy and other raw materials, one can only predict ever increasing competition for such resources and a drive to establish two closed economic zones — Japan, East and South-east Asia; Euro-Africa.

But need this be the only scenario? A gradual shift from resource- and-energy-intensive industry to knowledge-and-technology-intensive industry in the four industrialized states might lead to a complementarity with developing countries, which already exists in some industrial sectors. Such an international division of labour could be horizontal as well as vertical, with Japan and the European states agreeing to avoid unnecessary overlap and harmful duplication of effort in some regions, such as South-east Asia or Africa, and to act jointly or in parallel in others, such as the Middle East. There might also be consultation over burden-sharing as far as the absorption of the manufactured goods of the NICs is concerned, so that there is not, as now, the objection against an influx of the products of investment abroad by one country into the market of another.

Such an 'ideal' solution may appeal to Europeans and Japanese, but leaves out of account the interests of Third World countries. It would be a perfect model of the West's 'neo-imperialism' to which they object so strenuously — a new version of being the hewers of wood and drawers of water for the advanced economies. A Third World country cannot easily compete with the developed world in producing the infrastructure for heavy industry, but in knowledge-intensive industries it might have a better chance of starting on an equal level. The 'silicon valley' can be created at a rate determined primarily by the educational skills of the society in which it is located. Some of the new states, such as Singapore, are rapidly moving in this direction, so that a restructuring according to a division of labour as outlined above may not be the answer to the problems of the industrialized countries, and may only lead to more friction, both among themselves and with the Third World.

Thus, there is no easy solution to the complex problems of European/Japanese/Third World economic relationships. Unless the Western economies are restructured to meet the rising industrial competition from Third World countries, we are likely to see a sharpening of competition, both between Europe and Japan as well as between them and the NICs. On the other hand, restructuring to overcome competition from cheaper manufacturing industry in the Third World and heavy dependence on imported sources of energy and other primary materials, may be overtaken by the rapid technological development of some of the Third World countries, especially in the East Asian region, which would make nonsense of such an international division of labour.

As if this were not enough, it is also necessary to consider the part played by the United States as a major actor in the relations between the Third World and the West. Discussions of economic relations among the industrialized states are usually conducted in the context of trilateralism, with the United States forming the third side of the triangle. Until recently economic policies towards the Third World did not feature prominently in these discussions because the United States was largely self-sufficient in raw materials, and the potential for rivalry in Third World markets was not stressed. However, the gradual exhaustion of American reserves, notably of oil, have brought the United States increasingly into the field in search of primary materials. Moreover, the worst world depression since the 'great slump' has sharpened all forms of economic competition among the advanced countries.

The Superpowers and The Third World

American interest in the Third World cannot be divorced from American rivalry with the Soviet Union. United States policy, therefore, has a strategic as well as an economic dimension. Britain and France, as former imperial powers, shared American postwar strategic objectives in a very broad sense: Britain because of its long tradition of opposing Russian expansion in Asia, and France because of its concept as defender of the West in Indochina and North Africa against a communist-inspired global threat. It did not follow that they always saw eye to eye with the Americans. The latter, for example, were not convinced that the French served the Western interest by obstinately resisting the claims of Algerian nationalism. France and Britain, on the other hand, did not accept the view that China posed the major threat to Western interests in East Asia in the 1960s.

Both the deterioration of Western-Soviet relations in the 1970s and the onset of the most severe economic recession since the end of the Second World War greatly increased Western politico-strategic and economic preoccupations with the Third World. Their importance can be gauged from the agendas of the annual summit meetings of the leading industrialized states. Originally designed to deal primarily with trilateral economic relations, they have devoted more and more attention to global economic and political problems. The fact that the Western powers have similar economic and socio-political systems supports the argument for collaboration and coordination in devising political and economic strategies towards the rest of the world. There exist, however, at least equally important factors which pull in the opposite direction.

Under the Reagan Administration American policies are dominated by the objective of blocking and, where possible, rolling back the advance of Soviet influence. In theory there is no place for the nuances of international politics in such a strategy. The behaviour of Cuba or Vietnam, for instance, is equated with the behaviour of the Soviet Union, and the US indiscriminately supports all political and social forces that declare themselves to be anti-communist. This simplistic outlook is the consequence of a decade of frustrations and disappointments. Europeans and Japanese, on the other hand, have been reluctant to be identified with such a *Weltanschauung*, and their reactions to some of the activities of the Reagan Administration, as well as their initiatives, confirm the underlying differences in their approach.

Before turning to the policy implications of the differing European and Japanese interests, it is necessary to ask whether the Reagan Administration's assessment of the Soviet threat in the Third World is well founded, and whether in fact American rhetoric really fits

American practice.

Recent disagreements between the United States and its friends have not been over the *potential* danger of a Russian domination of Third World countries but over the nature and degree of that danger. One has to ask, for instance, to what extent Soviet influence in the world today is greater than it was twenty or thirty years ago. An interesting study by the independent Center for Defense Information in Washington published in January 1980,[7] came to the conclusion that although nineteen countries were under Soviet influence at the beginning of the 1980s, compared with seven in 1945, the peak of Soviet influence in the world was in the late 1950s. This result was achieved by comparing the percentages of countries under Soviet domination based on the total number of independent states at the time: 9 per cent of 70 states in 1945; 14 per cent of 91 states in the late 1950s; about 12 per cent of 157 states in 1980.

This is of course a rather simplistic way of calculating the degree of influence in the world. The authors of the study met the objection to an excessive reliance on numbers with an attempt to assess the importance of the countries under Russian influence. They used criteria of population, size, economic development, natural resources, military strength and regional importance as indices of power, according to ratings established by Ray Cline.[8] In terms of these, they could make a strong case for the actual decline of Soviet world influence, pointing to Yugoslavia, China, Indonesia and Egypt as examples where the Russians suffered serious setbacks over the years. They also stressed that the degree of influence has varied from country to country, reducing it to satellite status in some cases while promoting a tenuous alignment in others. Cline gave a zero power-rating to seven of the nineteen countries under various forms of Soviet domination (Afghanistan, Angola, Cambodia, Congo-Brazzaville, Laos, Mozambique, Southern Yemen). At best this is a very superficial analysis of power for an aggregate of national properties does not constitute power. It is the use made of national resources and the effect of that use which enable us to make a very rough calculus of a country's power in relation to the power of other countries.

Thus, in terms of natural resource potential, Angola and Mozambique should probably rate higher than, for instance, Bulgaria, which is given five points. Moreover, the strategic importance of both Angola and Mozambique, and of Southern Yemen, is surely considerable in the eyes of the Soviet Union. An examination of the location of some of these countries in relation to an expanding Soviet naval and airlift capability must give them a high rating in their potential for the exercise of Soviet power. For the purposes of estimating the degree of the Soviet advance in the world, the criteria established by Cline are of little use, and the authors of the study present a misleading picture when they dismiss the Soviet geopolitical momentum on the grounds that between one third and one half of the countries under the Soviet sway have a zero rating on Cline's scale.

The equation of Soviet influence is a combination of the resources and strategic location of a particular country with the Russian capability and will to exploit them. On this score it is undoubtedly useful if the Russians can enjoy basing facilities in Vietnam, Yemen, Ethiopia, Cuba and Angola. It is also useful for them to be able to use Cuban and Vietnamese troops, or East German and Czech 'technicians', to extend the Soviet sphere of influence. In so far as Afghanistan is a wedge between Pakistan and Iran and borders on the territory of the dissident Baluchis, it is of great strategic value because it may be the key to access to the Gulf. If one looks at the geographic distribution of Soviet centres of influence, there is considerable force in the argument that with positions in Syria, South Yemen and Ethiopia, as well as in Afghanistan, the Russians have at least as strong a position in the Middle Eastern and Gulf areas as they acquired when Egypt became their client state in the 1960s.

But they have lost Egypt since, and that is the important clue to the measurement of the Soviet geopolitical momentum. The authors of the study are correct when they stress the impermanence of Soviet influence. The Russians have retained unbroken control over six East European states and Mongolia since the end of the Second World War. Even there, however, Romania's independent foreign policy and the various upheavals in the German Democratic Republic, Hungary, Poland and Czechoslovakia have underlined the precarious nature of Soviet control. It is significant that of all the new states in the Third World, only Angola and Mozambique, two of the newest, have been in the Soviet sphere continuously since the beginning of their independence.

The fact of a shifting and constantly changing pattern of Soviet influence (Guinea, Iraq and Syria have each had two separate periods under Soviet influence) suggests two things: first, the Soviet Union is either not able or insufficiently ruthless to retain its control over a country once that country wants to discard its tutelage. The other and more important conclusion is that the governments of Third World countries exploit the Soviet connection for their own ends and have no hesitation in terminating it, regardless of ideological affinities. There is no reason to think that because Cuba and Vietnam appear to be willing proxies of the Soviet Union today, they will always be so.

The international alignments of the countries of the Third World are shaped by the opportunities offered to them by the rivalries of the major powers and by their own immediate interests and not by any ideological preference or sentimental attachments. Whatever the intentions of the Kremlin, Soviet global power and influence are conditioned by factors over which the Russians have at best imperfect control and often no control at all.

The same can be said of the United States. One need only refer to Israel's invasion of the Lebanon and the difficulties the United States has had in restraining its ally, to realise that if the Americans cannot control a country which is allegedly wholly dependent on the US for its basic security, how much more tenuous American influence is likely to be over countries which are not so beholden to it. Soviet failure in Egypt is paralleled by American failure in Iran. Elusiveness is one of the chief characteristics of the Third World.

But there is another factor which inhibits the superpowers: their restraint in dealing with each other. We may be fairly certain that once the United States has got over its current obsession about protecting Middle East oil from the Soviet Union, rolling forward into Afghanistan, and it becomes clear that the Soviet move was a police action and not aimed at the region's oil reserves, Soviet-American relations in the Middle East will settle down again. Indeed, the restrained Soviet policy during the Lebanese crisis in the summer of 1982 is further proof of superpower caution.

The rhetoric of the first flush of political victory — a victory won partly because of the promise of a more vigorous anti-communist and anti-Soviet policy — has given way, as so often in the past, to a pragmatic and cautious policy, covered by periodic bursts of the old fire to cheer up the supporters back home. Even in its dealings with avowedly communist states, the United States has preferred cool calculations to ideological fervour. On balance, the strategic relationship with communist China has carried more weight than the commitment to Nationalist Taiwan. In spite of President Reagan's avowed support of the latter and his apparent willingness to see some deterioration in the relationship with the People's Republic of China so painfully built up by previous administrations, there was a limit beyond which it would have been imprudent to go. The agreement which ended the dispute over continued American arms sales to Taiwan was face-saving for both sides, but the US had to concede that China has the last word over the

Europe, Japan and the Third World

future of the island.[9]

All this does not alter the fact that the principal strategic objective of the United States is to counter and if possible reduce Soviet influence in the Third World. It follows that in its policies, however idealistic they may be, strategic calculations can never be wholly absent. Whatever a President may have committed himself to do, the machinery of government has a built-in tendency to correct any bias which deviates too far from or threatens the basic objective. This is what happened to Carter's human rights programme, and it is happening again with Reagan's anti-communist zeal.

The pursuit of great-power politics is irrelevant to the interests of the European states and Japan. They are no longer imperial powers in the traditional sense, and their interest in the Third World is to have freedom of access to its raw materials and its markets. The developing countries are inclined to regard this as a euphemism for 'neo-imperialism', in which more subtle pressures are exercised to impose the 'freedom of access'. None the less, except in a few and declining number of instances, they (Britain and France — Germany and Japan not at all) do not have the option of a military intervention to protect this interest. They have to be sensitive to the shifting politics and mood of a developing country and their impact on its economy.

This can lead to contradictions between a preference for free trade and the *status quo* on the one hand, and adjustment to the demands of the producer countries on the other. Thus, while the market economy may require a reduction of output of a particular commodity or a lowering of prices, developing countries dependent on selling their minerals in a limited market, as in the case of many suppliers of copper concentrate who are heavily dependent on Japan, may demand artificial measures such as stockpiling or the ban on exports of processed materials in order to maintain a certain price level. The demands may be accompanied by the threat of expropriation if they are not met. Zaire used such an implicit threat of nationalizing Japanese investments if Japan failed to uphold the price of copper.

Where a developing country has lurched into the pro-Soviet camp, or at least away from the 'West', relations may, none the less continue and even expand. One thinks of the export of North Vietnamese coal to Japan and of British Leyland trucks to Cuba. For Europe and Japan, therefore, relations with the Third World are not dictated primarily by the political orientation of a particular country but by the mutuality of their economic interests.

That this need not be a one-way traffic — the Western states adjusting to the whims of the developing country — was illustrated by Mozambique's agreement with the Federal Republic of Germany. For more than four years Mozambique had sought a loan from EEC, but was foiled by the Federal Republic's veto because of its refusal to subscribe to the description of West Berlin preferred by the West Germans. In August 1982 Mozambique finally accepted the nomenclature of 'Land Berlin', instead of the 'Berlin (West)' which is used by the Warsaw Pact countries, thus signifying recognition of its position as a state of the Federal Republic. As a result, Mozambique may join the Lomé Convention; a clear case where economic interests have weakened a political alignment.[10]

Prospects for Collaboration

In the past few years there have been some signs that Europeans and Japanese are aware of a congruence of interests outside their immediate regions; the Japanese rather more so than the Europeans. This is not surprising. The enormous expansion of the Japanese economy has underlined Japan's vulnerability. Of course, within its neighbourhood in North-east Asia, Japan is closely tied to the United States, but elsewhere Japanese interests can no longer be safeguarded by giving verbal and, in the UN, voting support to the United States. Hence the search for new orientations.

The West Europeans have been progressing in the opposite direction. They are turning inwards, and even the former imperial powers have ceased to stress their 'role' or 'mission' in the world. Instead, they confine their attention primarily to Europe and its backyards: the Middle East and Africa. They see Japan as just another threat to their precarious economic stability, though they welcome Japanese investment provided it helps to create more jobs. In the Third World they may be open to some loose coordination with Japanese enterprises, but generally think of them as competitors.

The Iran hostage crisis of 1979/80 and the Russian occupation of Afghanistan have led if not to active co-operation then at least to a convergence which has so far been hardly noticed on the European side. The crises provided opportunities for collaboration over relations with both superpowers.

Japan joined general criticism of the abortive attempt to free the hostages by military action and complained that the Americans had kept their allies in the dark. In April 1980, Mr Ōkita was sent to the meeting of the Community's foreign ministers in Luxembourg, and it was emphasised that this signified Japan's wish to increase co-operation with EEC over important international *political* issues. The Japanese ambassador was recalled from Tehran in concert with similar action by the members of EEC. A senior Japanese Foreign Ministry official was reported as saying that 'The Government will let the ambassador return to Tehran on the same day when the ambassadors of the EC (sic) countries do so'.[11] In May 1980 Prime Minister Ōhira attended the funeral of Marshal Tito in Belgrade, and then went on to Bonn for informal talks with Chancellor Schmidt to discuss the role of Japan and the West European states in reducing international tensions.

Later in the year the President of the European Commission, M. Gaston Thorn, visited Tokyo, and agreed with his hosts on the need for closer co-operation between the Community and Japan and the need to be aware of their 'common responsibilities'.

All are words which have to be translated into deeds, but they are interesting pointers none the less. A more material form of coordination was the decision of Japan and the Federal Republic of Germany to strengthen Turkey in the wake of the Soviet invasion of Afghanistan, by providing it with special economic assistance, although the Germans had taken the initiative in asking Japan to share in this enterprise.

Another example of overlapping interests is the support of EEC for ASEAN. In this case the Europeans are concerned with a region where the Japanese have declared a special interest, and their action has undoubtedly had the tacit approval if not encouragement of the government in Tokyo. At the second meeting of ASEAN and EEC foreign ministers in Kuala Lumpur in March 1980 (the first had been held in Brussels in November 1978), a separate political declaration was issued at Malaysia's request, in which the two parties supported each other's positions over Kampuchea, refugees from Indochina, and the Afghanistan question. The last two paragraphs referred to the two groupings as areas of stability in their regions.[13]

Parallel to various political moves which have been chiefly confined to declarations of intent rather than specific action, there are also indications of economic co-operation in the Third World. So far, the accelerating rate of Japanese overseas investment reflects three basic objectives: the need for guaranteed access to natural resources; a search for cheaper labour; and the securing of markets. Such a development has been met with the charge of neo-colonialism, not only in the developing world but also in the industrialized countries of Europe where Japanese investment has tried to bypass the effect of rising protectionism.

In March 1981 the Japan Machinery Exporters' Association and the British Engineering Employers' Federation reached an agreement to promote large-scale joint projects in South-east Asia, the Middle East and Africa, while the British Government undertook to examine the possibility of amending its financing and export insurance systems in the interest of these projects.[14] Such a venture will not remove the charge of neo-colonialism levelled by the poor nations against the rich, especially as they are already a common feature of the activities of the multinational companies, but the promotion of this kind of enterprise between the industries of two countries in association with their governments is a further step in European-Japanese coordination.

In order to be effective in the long term and not be mere responses to a passing fashion in international relations, the Europeans and Japanese must address the question of the overriding purpose of their collaboration in the Third World. This includes a consideration of its strategic implications: what is the problem and what is the 'threat' to the development of fruitful relationships with the Third World? Is it Soviet expansionism or is it the volatile condition of the Third World stemming from its poverty, social instability, and political sensitivity to the threat of new imperialisms?

If the principal problem is to meet the Soviet 'threat', then Europeans and Japanese must not only coordinate their policies to meet it, but coordinate them with the United States and, because of its military strength, accept its leadership here as well as in their own regions. If, however, the crucial issue is the condition of the Third World, which incidentally consists of a mass of states ranging from the extremely rich to the appallingly poor, then Europeans and Japanese must focus on their relations with those countries as distinct from and perhaps free from any superpower alignments.

Ironically, superpower rivalry in the Third World has a double effect. It is a source of destabilization in so far as one superpower will be tempted to support and exploit subversion against a government which is supported by the other. The United States has sought to undermine the regimes in Angola and Kampuchea by directly or indirectly supporting various guerrilla movements, some of which, such as the Khmer Rouge, profess the very ideology against which the United States is on crusade. Similarly, the Russians support revolutionary movements or dissidents in El Salvador and Oman. All this can lead to further contradictions. Thus, we have a marxist government defending the interests of 'monopoly capitalism' in the shape of multinational oil companies, such as operate in Kabinda, against the assaults or threats from pro-Western forces.

On the other hand, superpower domination may also have the effect of stabilizing a country, making it a more reliable partner in economic relations with countries from the opposite camp. The Japanese, for instance, can do good and profitable business with Vietnam and North Korea, regardless of the colour or allegiance of their regimes. British Leyland, too, found Cuba after the revolution a most lucrative market for its buses and lorries.

Soviet influence over the regimes of resource-rich countries is unlikely to lead to a cut-off of supplies to bring the West to its knees. That would be not only a crude but also a self-defeating exercise, for it would run counter to the interests of the producers who need the markets of the industrialized world, and often depend on its capital and technology to maintain and enhance production. Russian pressure might, however, take a more subtle form by encouraging the client state to sell to the West, and then use its earnings to pay for goods and arms from the Soviet Union. It might also seek control over key resources, let us say the oil fields of the Middle East, as a means with which to blackmail the West into providing assistance in the development of its own resources: 'we will let you have what you want in return for your capital and technical assistance in developing the oil and gas fields of Siberia'.

Given their dependence for at least the next decade on the oil of the Middle East, the West European states and Japan would be particularly vulnerable to such forms of pressure. They also have an incentive to become less dependent on the United States, for past experience has shown that when the squeeze is on, the American-based oil companies will first cut supplies to other countries before they reduce the flow to the United States.

In sum, the interests of Europe and Japan coincide on the politico-strategic level but not necessarily on the economic plane. They have no wish to see the Third World divided into mutually exclusive spheres of influence by the superpowers. They want to see it as open as possible, with countries free to choose their economic partners regardless of their ideological colour. They have every interest in preventing the process of global alliance-building by the Soviet Union and the United States. An untidy world may be an uncertain world, but it enables one to be more flexible and provides more room for manoeuvre.

Economic co-operation, in fact, may be better organized outside the framework of interstate relations. For instance, a British manufacturer incorporating Japanese microelectronics in agricultural-processing equipment for a co-operative having East German advisers in a Marxist-orientated Third World country, might do much better business than if he had to wait for decisions from all four governments that were indirectly involved.

European and Japanese economic co-operation at macro-level may be desirable in theory but, apart from some specific instances, is difficult to put into practice. For one thing, the requirements of each state are different. At one extreme is Japan with its almost total dependence on imported sources of energy and other primary materials. At the other end is Britain, self-sufficient in energy and, with appropriate technology, potentially self-sufficient in food. France and Germany are somewhere in between, with the former nearer the British end and the latter nearer the Japanese end of the spectrum.

Furthermore, a system where Europeans, Japanese, Americans and Russians compete for their favours is infinitely preferable to resource-rich countries than any cartel-like agreements among the industrialized societies to divide the Third World between them in order to avoid competition and friction. Such co-operation, however well intentioned it might be, is bound to smack of economic imperialism. The countries of the Third World will want to play the Japanese off against the Europeans and both against the Americans and the West against the East, in order to secure the best terms for themselves.

This leaves out the fate of the least developed countries (LDCs), those which have no significant resources to offer. As they sink ever deeper into poverty and debt, there is a case for European and Japanese co-operation in assisting these countries, not for any economic advantage, for there may be none, but on moral and humanitarian grounds. Such an approach calls for a concept of international responsibility which does not rest on national or commercial self-interest alone. It raises the question of what kind of world-order Europeans and Japanese want to see established. Their answer will obviously reflect their interests, but those very interests may also require an element of vision. In the absence of such a vision they are likely to embark on a new drive for domination of the weaker states, which can only result in severe conflicts among themselves and with the developing world.

Notes

1. Energy supply targets for the fiscal year 1990, as set by the Japanese

Government in April 1982 (*Japan*, London, Embassy of Japan Information Centre), no. 196, 15 July 1982.

2. *Japan Times*, 8 January 1980; *Japan Times Weekly*, 27 November 1982.

3. *Japan*, (London, Embassy of Japan Information Centre), no. 149, 1 July 1981.

4. This is true of official policy rather than of public opinion in Japan. A poll conducted by the Prime Minister's office at the end of July 1975 revealed that 67% of the respondents thought highly of economic aid; of whom 31% said that assistance of the poor by the rich was a 'human obligation', 19% said such aid was useful for world peace and only 17% said that it was economically advantageous to Japan. (*Japan Times Weekly*, 8 November 1975).

5. *Japan* (London, Embassy of Japan Information Centre), no. 149, 1 July 1981.

6. See 'Japan's High-Tech Challenge', *Newsweek*, 9 August 1982, pp. 20-36.

7. 'Soviet Geopolitical Momentum: Myth or Menace?' (The *Defense Monitor*, Washington, DC, Center for Defense Information, vol. IX no. 1, January 1980).

8. Ray Cline, *World Power Trends* (Washington, DC, Westview Press Inc., in association with Georgetown University, 1980).

9. The joint communiqué of 17 August 1982, stated that the US and China had agreed on a 'fundamental policy aimed at the peaceful reunification of China'. American arms sales to Taiwan are not to exceed quantitatively and qualitatively those since the normalization of relations between Washington and Beijing. The US also promised a gradual reduction of sales, leading to a final resolution of the issue over a period of time. Observers have pointed out that this last vague stipulation leaves the issue uncertain and may eventually give rise to further difficulties: *Guardian*, 18 August 1982.

10. *Guardian*, 10 August 1982.

11. *Japan Times Weekly*, 26 April 1980. See also *Japan* (Embassy of Japan Information Centre, London), no. 96, 23 April 1980.

12. *Japan* (Embassy of Japan Information Centre, London), no. 118, 15 October 1980.

13. *Europa Archiv*, 35th Year, no. 8, 25 April 1980, pp. D195-8.

14. *Japan* (Embassy of Japan Information Centre, London), no. 137, 11 March 1981.

6 EUROPE'S AND JAPAN'S CHOICES

It is the main purpose of this final chapter to examine alternative courses open to Western Europe and Japan in an international system dominated by the superpowers, and to end with a recommendation of the course which I believe holds out the best promise for the establishment of a peaceful international order.

Relations with the Superpowers

There are two outstanding features in the special relationship of Western Europe and Japan with the United States. They are tied to America because of a real, or at least perceived need to have an American guarantee of their security. The other feature is their identification with the 'West'. It is from this identification that there spring many of the values which, it is felt, can only be secured through alliance with the US, though that is not to deny that security in itself is also a value.

The 'West' can be defined on two levels, leaving aside the purely geographical meaning which is an absurdity in the context of this book. At the one level it refers to a cultural tradition that evolved in Europe from Graeco/Roman and Judaeo/Christian roots. It was transferred to the United States, where it is the dominant cultural influence, and was spread around the world in the age of European imperialism. The Russians have shared in the tradition through the influence of the Orthodox Church, the impact of the partly non-Russian elites that dominated the state in the eighteenth and nineteenth centuries, and the characteristic Western messianism of the prevailing communist ideology. The thinking of Marx and Engels was, after all, a product of the Western tradition. Nevertheless, Russia has always stood somewhat apart from the mainstream of European history and civilization, and its historic relations with Europe bear a resemblance to Japan's relations with the Asian mainland. Europeans have tended to regard Russia as not fully part of their civilization, just as the Chinese have vacillated between including Japan within the ambit of their universe and regarding it as a land beyond its bounds.

On the second level of definition, the West may be described as a collection of pluralist societies which are not dominated by a single orthodoxy to the exclusion of all others. In each country there is freedom for contending social, economic, political and religious doctrines, with generally recognized and accepted procedures for the transfer of political power at regular intervals through general elections by secret ballot.

It is obvious that the first definition applies to Europe and the United States and such essentially 'European' countries as Canada, Australia and New Zealand. However, it has become very difficult to define the West on the basis of cultural tradition or ethnic composition. Indeed, the West in this sense is on the decline and the definition increasingly meaningless. The superior technology and organization on which its domination of the world rested in the past is now in possession of other societies, including Japan, China, and the emerging Third World powers such as India and Nigeria, which do not share the same cultural roots and specifically reject the concept of the West so defined. Moreover, Western Europe and the United States have become multi-ethnic and multicultural societies which make cultural exclusiveness untenable.

Thus, any meaningful definition of the West has to be confined to societies which have shared social and political values and the structures which embody them. Here is the common ground between the United States, Western Europe and Japan – and other non-European countries. The traditional West may have given birth to many of these values, but they can no longer be regarded as exclusive to a particular ethnic group or geographical region.

Although the Euro-American relationship is more intimate for historical reasons than the Euro-American relationship with Japan, there is substantial common ground between Europe, America and Japan in terms of values and political structures. Europe and Japan also have a common interest *vis-à-vis* the United States.

Because of the mixture of power politics and ideological confrontation between the United States and the Soviet Union, the Americans are inclined to categorize all those on their side in the conflict as belonging to the West, often referred to as the 'Free World'. This classification becomes ridiculous when one looks around the world at some of America's friends. It is therefore in the interests of the European states and Japan to define the West in such a way as not to make a mockery of the word 'free', but it is even more in their interest not to allow the United States to dictate 'East-West' relations in such simplistic ideological terms.

The relations of Western Europe and Japan with the Soviet Union are more straightforward because of the absence of the kind of intimate association which characterizes their relationship with the United States. The central problem is how to live at peace with the giant neighbour without succumbing to its political and ideological embrace. This implies a security policy which has hitherto been predicated on the American guarantee. The question whether the dependence on the US should continue, and if so in what form, will be discussed later.

If security represents the negative aspect of the relationship with Russia, then the development of economic intercourse may be considered its positive aspect. Western capital and technology are needed to help in the development of Russia's vast natural wealth. Siberia is the world's greatest untapped area in this respect. It contains about three-quarters of the Soviet Union's mineral, fuel and energy resources, and about half its timber reserves. With the passage of time, both the Russian and East European economies will become increasingly dependent on these resources.[1] As the projects for the supply of natural gas illustrate, West Europe, and eventually Japan when the exploitation of eastern Siberia gets under way, will also benefit from their development. Since it would be a great advantage to have Western assistance in this vast enterprise, the Russians have a strong incentive to allow Europeans and Japanese to take a share of the resources in return for the hard currencies needed to purchase foreign goods and technology. A mutual economic interest thus links the Soviet Union with its neighbours and may become increasingly important to both in the future.

Policy Directions

In the light of the various priorities in their relations with both superpowers, several questions face Europeans and Japanese as they contemplate the future. Is it in their interest to continue allowing the United States to have a virtual monopoly of defining what is meant by the West and, by implication, dictating the course of East-West relations? Are the security structures which have been developed since the war still appropriate to their interests? Should good-neighbourly relations with the Soviet Union be strengthened and developed beyond the economic and technological dimension with the object of eventually making it a partner in promoting international security? Finally, what are the prospects for European-Japanese collaboration in working out the answers to these questions?

I believe that Japan and the states of Western Europe have the choice of following one of three directions. They may go along with the present drift in world politics and allow themselves to be gradually integrated into a global alliance which is led, if not dominated, by the United States. Alternatively, they may seek to break with the American connection and resort to neutralism or non-alignment, or the construction of new independent power blocs. A third option would include the retention of a modified security relationship with the United States and the attempt at a new definition of the West, which would reject the Soviet ideological system but would at the same time refuse to accept an East-West ideological struggle on the grounds that ideology is a poor and dangerous basis on which to deal with the problems of an exceedingly complex and interdependent world. Instead, it would focus on the development of business-like relations with the Soviet Union, governed by interest and the concentration on particular issues. An additional objective would be to reduce the military dimension in the relationship with both superpowers.

A Global Alliance

The drift in world politics, and especially the policies of the two superpowers in the early 1980s, is towards the construction of two competing alliance systems. The Soviet Union has achieved a rough strategic parity with the United States and has broken out of its periphery, acquiring client states in all the continents. Non-alignment retains its attraction for the Third World, but has lost its impetus. The founding fathers, Tito, Nehru, Nasser and others have died, and it is a strange sort of 'non-alignment' that includes Cuba as one of the movement's leaders. The United States can no longer act as policeman of the world, and among its friends there is one state, Japan, which is beginning to rival its economic strength, and another group of states, the European Community, which could become an economic giant. Outside the Western 'alliance' new powers of great potential are beginning to emerge. They include China, India, Nigeria and Brazil.

All these developments could be taken to indicate a fragmentation of power, and this was certainly the meaning attached to them in the early 1970s. Events in the past few years could also be interpreted as underlining the increasingly complex structure of power relationships, but may in fact point towards a new bipolarity in world politics.

The annual meetings of the leaders of the major industrialized states, with the President of the European Community in attendance, have shifted their attention from purely economic to political problems. Japanese officials have begun regular consultations on political and security matters with officials from NATO. The Soviet-Vietnamese Treaty of Friendship and Co-operation (1978) and the inclusion of Vietnam and Cuba into Comecon, as well as the substantial presence of Cuban troops in Angola and Ethiopia, signal the establishment of a global alliance led by the Soviet Union. The Sino-Japanese Treaty of Peace and Friendship (1978), the normalization of Sino-American relations (1979), and the tacit military collaboration between the United States and China have pointed to a tripartite line-up in North-east Asia. Add to this the drawing closer together of the members of ASEAN in the face of Vietnamese domination of Cambodia and Laos, and their ties with Japan, and we have in existence a number of links which could be forged into two alliance systems that face each other across the world.

There are, of course, many cross-currents and contradictions on both sides. The Russians find it difficult to hold together their allies in the face of local animosities or the opportunism of Third World states. A choice had to be made between Ethiopia and Somalia. Egypt broke its ties of dependence on the Soviet Union. The management of the diverse nations of Eastern Europe is a source of constant anxiety in the Kremlin. The West is inhibited from associating with its 'natural' allies — Israel and South Africa — and China has given clear indications that it intends to play an independent role in world politics. Moreover, there are many issues over which the allies of the United States are at loggerheads. The conflict between Argentina and Britain is a recent example of such antagonisms. But there is little doubt that the interest of the superpowers is to dragoon their friends into a solid phalanx of opposition against each other.

Such a trend is potentially very dangerous because the logic of bipolar confrontation leads to a trial of strength which, in the present circumstances, would mean a contest for world domination. For obvious reasons the United States and the Soviet Union exercise considerable restraint in their mutual relationship, so that their battles are fought indirectly and by proxy in the lands and among the peoples of other countries. Nevertheless, the danger of a third world war cannot be dismissed out of hand, however unlikely it may seem today.[2] Historical parallels, especially with the period before the First World War, spring readily to mind. Chancellor Schmidt spoke of Sarajevo at the time of the Russian invasion of Afghanistan, and the resemblance does not necessarily end there.

On the other hand, awareness of the past and changes in military technology have so altered conditions that it would be dangerously misleading to think that the past would simply repeat itself. Instead, the real dangers may lie elsewhere. The risk that things will get out of control because of the long lead-times required for the mobilization and assembly of armies, and that as a consequence military necessity will take over before the pursuit of a diplomatic solution to a crisis had been exhausted, has been replaced by the risk of not acting fast enough or of accidental action in an age when instant readiness is of the essence.

Attempts at the demarcation of spheres of influence have been a feature of the superpower relationship in the past: through Dulles's doctrine of massive retaliation; after the establishment of the two German states; as a result of the Cuban missile crisis; and through various treaties, of which the Soviet-Vietnamese Treaty is the most recent example. A new demarcation today would only differ from previous arrangements in its comprehensive and global character. But even if it could be worked out, it would be inherently unstable.

Historical evidence suggests that power rivalries are not appeased by this method. There will aways be the temptation to seize any opportunity to nibble away at one's opponent's sphere and expand one's own. The ancient Roman and Persian Empires were doing it all the time in their shadowy borderlands in Asia Minor. A global division could not possibly be absolute, and there would always be weak spots where allegiance to one or other of the two camps would be ambivalent and invite interference.

The system would also be inherently unstable because of the ideological dimension of the superpower rivalry. The Soviet Union professes an eschatological ideology, and all its actions are justified in the name of 'the cause'. In terms of their ideology, the Soviets cannot accept an indefinite freezing of the world into two camps. Their conception of historical destiny must triumph, and they will disguise from their opponents and from themselves the real motives which impel them in their quest for world dominion. The United States professes to stand for a supreme human value, 'freedom', which is threatened by the Marxist philosophy of the Soviet Union. Hence the propensity to include any opponent of Marxism in the 'Free World'. We have thus the classic confrontation of the irresistible force with the immovable barrier.

In the *real* world, of course, there is plenty of contradiction, plenty of opportunism and plenty of compromise in the policies of the superpowers. But instead of recognizing the inevitability and even the desirability of such 'imperfections', they try to persuade themselves and their publics that these are only necessary tactical manoeuvres dictated by specific circumstances, which do not deflect them from the ultimate purpose: the triumph of this creed and the destruction of the enemy's creed.

It does not take much foresight, therefore, to forecast that sooner or later the world is likely to become engulfed in a more general conflict between the superpowers. It may not start formally with the declarations and acts of war that preceded the two previous world wars, but could grow almost imperceptibly out of a gradual merging of a number of scattered local conflicts.

Let us suppose, for example, that the Russians become increasingly frustrated in their attempts to control Afghanistan, making no headway in pacifying the countryside and suffering a steady draining of their manpower and equipment from the harassment of tribesmen armed and supplied by the West, Iran, Pakistan and China. They may then decide to intervene in Iran to take advantage of the unstable situation there and to support their friends, but also to remove one source of support for the Mojahadin of Afghanistan. In the course of this operation the situation in Afghanistan would be linked more directly with the situaion in the Gulf region and the Iran-Iraq war. This, in turn, might have repercussions on the conflict between Israel and the Arabs. There would be anxiety about the flow of Middle East oil to the Western countries and about NATO's southern flank and the security of Turkey.

The ever-widening web of hostilities, even if the superpowers are not at first in direct confrontation, is bound to increase tensions and apprehensions. If this happened after earlier attempts to stake out their respective spheres of influence, the situation would be all the more dangerous. The mutual testing of determination would increase the pressure for some military demonstration to make one's point. The possibility of a direct confrontation between Soviet and American armed forces, with incalculable consequences, could not be ruled out. At one stage a limited use of nuclear weapons might even be decided upon, partly because of their incorporation in war-fighting capabilities and partly because it would be easier to justify their use as weapons aimed at purely military targets in the sparsely populated desert regions of the Middle East than in the densely populated and urbanized region of Central Europe.

It may be objected that such scenarios depend too much on extrapolations of historical experience, and that the relations between the superpowers are a new genus of international politics. After all, in spite of severe crises which in earlier times would have led to the outbreak of war, there has been no war between nuclear weapon states since 1945, if we leave out the border skirmishes between the Soviet Union and a nascent nuclear China at the end of the 1960s. This is true, and there may be no direct armed conflict between the United States and the Soviet Union for many years to come. Nuclear deterrence may impose a strict discipline on all military conflicts in the future, and 1945 may have marked the end of the epoch of mass warfare ushered in by the French Revolution and the Napoleonic Wars. Perhaps we are back in an age of circumscribed military activity in the pursuit of limited objectives.

Against this one must set the ambition of empires which know no bounds until they are created by an even stronger external opposition or internal decay; one must set the driving force of ideological perceptions; and one must set the vertical and horizontal proliferation of nuclear weapons which has made them less distinguishable from other 'conventional' weapons and which is creating new centres of decision over their use, all the more difficult to coordinate and control in a severe crisis.

An unequivocal incorporation of Western Europe and Japan into a bipolar system might seem natural because, as has been argued throughout this book, if a choice has to be made between the United States and the Soviet Union, Europeans and Japanese must throw in their lot with the Americans. In essence, therefore, we would be returning to the posture of the late 1940s and the 1950s, whose main objective was the containment of Soviet expansion. However, this time America's allies would be expected to shoulder more of the common burden and some of them would no longer be confined to regional roles. In a sense it would be a return to what happened during the Korean War, when fifteen countries from all round the world participated on the side of the United Nations. For the most part the contributions were symbolic rather than substantial, and were in any case only for the duration of the fighting.

When the United States was anxious to mount a similar common effort in Vietnam in the late 1960s, the response was much weaker; a clear indication of the extent to which the international system was changing. Today, however, the major allies of the United States are prepared to pay at least lip-service to the need for a common effort to contain the Russians, as demonstrated by the declarations issued from the summits of the Western industrial countries in Venice (1980) and Ottawa (1981).

If the four major industrial states were to follow this path and gradually become integrated into an American-led global alliance system, it would be a sure way towards confrontation with the Soviet bloc. Such a course would not necessarily lead to a set-piece war from the familiar pattern of the first half of this century. More likely would be a pattern of sporadic but increasingly frequent armed conflicts all over the world, involving the superpowers and their principal allies in various ways, but leading to no clear conclusions. Thus, there would be created a kind of permanent atmosphere of crisis with a corresponding development of garrison-state and siege mentalities, such as already exist in the Soviet Union and other totalitarian societies. The implications of this scenario were spelled out by George Orwell in *Nineteen Eighty-four*.[3]

That remarkable satirist and prophet has gained most attention for his uncanny forecast of the technological revolution which would make possible the world of 'Big Brother'. Less attention has been paid to his detailed account of the emergence of three superstates and their relationship of perpetual war. The never-ending conflict on the outer marches of these empires and over certain areas which none of them controls permanently, leads to no decisive results, but creates a climate of tension and war hysteria without, however, affecting the ordinary run of people's drab and regimented lives. Orwell's scenario of the embattled superstates of Oceania, Eurasia and Eastasia might also correspond to the shape of things to come if Europe and Japan opted for the second response to the present drift of events.

New Blocs or Neutralism

This would be the opposite to integration into a global alliance. It would be marked by a withdrawal from association with the United States into neutralist or non-aligned policies, or the attempt to create power blocs that would eventually rival the superpowers. The potential for such policies exists in each of the four countries. There are strong elements which have always opposed the American connection, which they would call 'domination'. They are not confined to the communists and left-wing socialists. Indeed, Labour governments in Britain and socialist governments in France, especially since the inauguration of President Mitterand, have tended to display greater enthusiasm for the Atlantic Alliance than have their conservative opponents.

Gaullist-style nationalism, the partly open and partly hidden nationalism of the Japanese right and left, the nationalism of Enoch Powell and the populist little-Englander attitude of large sections of the Labour Party, are all potent forces which would loosen the ties with the

United States, though their policies might be full of contradictions and irreconcilable objectives. Gaullism took a nationalist stance precisely because it reckoned that France could count on American protection against the Soviet Union. The Japanese nationalists will support the Mutual Security Treaty system as a cover under which Japan can rearm and grow strong. Enoch Powell's brand of English nationalism can flourish only if the Americans keep the international peace. The policies of the Labour Party call for a nuclear-free Britain but membership of the Atlantic Alliance.

What adds strength to all these brands of anti-American sentiment and the alternative policies that go with them is the economic friction with the United States. Until the late 1960s the United States was not only the greatest but also the dominant economic power in the West. Today it is still the strongest economic power but no longer dominant. Indeed, the so-called economic challenge from the United States with its threat to take over European industry, which so exercised M. Servan-Schreiber[4] and many other Europeans in the 1960s, has turned out to be a blessing. It poured capital into the European economy and therefore helped to make it strong. American procurements in Japan, especially during the Korean and Vietnamese wars, also played an important part in the expansion of Japanese industries.

The impact of American economic policies thus ironically laid the foundations for the strength and independence of the European and Japanese economies. None the less, in times of recession the basic interdependence of the three economies becomes apparent very quickly. We hear nothing of the danger of American domination of European industry; only demands for more American investment to help meet the problem of unemployment and complaints about high interest rates in the United States because of their damaging effects on the European and Japanese economies. However, as the current recession is prolonged, trade wars and the pressure for protectionism are becoming major factors in weakening the cohesion of the West.

A general move away from the United States might take various forms. It could lead to the promotion of new power blocs – A West European bloc and a Japanese-East Asian bloc, both of which are already in an embryonic state. The formation of some kind of European-Japanese 'alliance' is a less likely prospect because of the physical separation of the two regions and the disparity between their political and strategic situations. The security problems of Western Europe and Japan are parallel but not identical.

If a direct link between West Europe and Japan is beyond the reach of practical policies, another form of independent bloc-building might be the attempt to forge closer links with a particular developing region. Thus, one can imagine a linkage between Europe and Africa and between Japan, China and South-east Asia.

Such North-South connections have their obvious attractions and, though not much discussed these days, have been mooted for some time. It is argued that a close economic relationship between a highly industrialized region and a group of developing countries would be of great mutual advantage. Against this is the obvious objection of the developing countries that such an arrangement would be nothing less than the recreation of empires in which they would provide the raw materials and manpower for their masters.

Strong economic ties already exist through the Lomé Convention, between the Common Market and many of the countries which once belonged to the British and French Empires, and between Japan and the member states of ASEAN. As we saw in Chapter 5, the trend towards such bloc-building is reinforced by patterns of import dependence, investment flows and official aid. However, these relations are politically very sensitive, as illustrated by ASEAN's growing unease over Japan's economic domination of the region and the possible effect of Sino-Japanese economic collaboration. There is also a wide gap between the Francophone and Anglophone countries of Africa that would have to be overcome before one could think of the grander regional associations.

An alternative form of withdrawal from an American-dominated alliance structure would be the adoption of neutrality on the Swiss model. This might be accomplished by individual states – it has some popular appeal in Japan, whose geographical isolation would also favour such a course. Alternatively, neutrality might be sought through blocs. ASEAN's original objective, for example, was to establish a Zone of Peace, Freedom and Neutrality (ZOPFAN).

Neutrality does not necessarily imply weakness or passivity, or even indifference. Switzerland is a well-armed state, jealous of its sovereignty and determined to defend its independence. Its neutrality involves a clear and well-defined policy: no entanglement with any kind of alliance – hence its refusal to join the United Nations because it was born out of the wartime alliance against the Axis powers; a readiness to play host to all kinds of international agencies; to provide a meeting place for international negotiations, to be used as an intermediary in conflict situations; and to serve as humanitarian agent in war. Nor has Switzerland stood apart from international economic organizations, as is testified by its membership of EFTA and of the OECD.

However, the kind of neutrality associated with Switzerland may be difficult to apply to the four countries of this study because of their entanglements with world politics and the practical difficulties in the way of cutting loose from them. Not least, there would have to be a substantial change in the habits of official and popular thinking about the 'role' of one's country, something which would be very difficult for Europeans but perhaps less so for Japanese.

The weight and influence of large states almost inevitably makes them important actors in world politics, so that non-alignment might be thought of as a better option.[5] Neutrality and non-alignment are not the same thing. The former stems from a concept in international law, though, as suggested, it can mean something more than non-participation in a war between other countries. Non-alignment, on the other hand, is a concept of foreign policy stemming from a decision not to become involved in the confrontation between East and West. It is a negative policy towards the alliances led by the superpowers, and a positive policy largely reflecting the needs and aspirations of the developing countries of the Third World. For this reason, the non-aligned group of states does not include any of the traditionally neutral countries, though some of them, such as Sweden, might be regarded as combining the status of neutrality with a non-aligned policy. In spite of its formal neutrality, Sweden has not hesitated to take a forthright stand on particular international issues, as, for example, in its opposition to American policy over Vietnam.

Neutral and non-aligned countries, individually and in groups, have played an active and positive role in world politics. Neither neutralism nor non-alignment would lead to the development of a multipolar balance of power system, because the concepts of neutrality and non-alignment specifically reject alliances as instruments of policy. However, the idea of non-alignment might be more appealing to Europeans because it does not have the passive connotation of neutrality.

In all four countries there exist important sections of public opinion receptive to the idea of either loosening or breaking the ties with the United States. There is, however, no agreement over the alternative to the existing alliance policy. Some advocate a retreat into neutralism or non-alignment, others dream of establishing new centres of power.

The effect of such policies would be to reduce the danger of becoming entangled in a global-alliance system dominated by the United States. However, neutralism, whatever form it took, would expose the state to Soviet pressures or blackmail as a result of the withdrawal of

American protection. Creating new power blocs to compete with the superpowers would start a process leading to the Orwellian syndrome of three or four competing 'empires'. Thus, neither course would serve the interest of security or the establishment of a peaceful international order.

Basic Security and Constructive Policies

This option aims to achieve both of the last-mentioned objectives. It would mitigate the danger of the current struggle between the two camps by avoiding incorporation into a global alliance; it does not seek to enter the power game independently, but equally eschews withdrawal into isolation. It has two major components: the provision of basic national security and the promotion of positive policies designed to create a new international order.

The key problem for Western Europe and Japan is security, a problem with a psychological as well as a physical dimension. There is no serious evidence that the Russians would invade Western Europe or the countries of North-east Asia at the earliest opportunity. No doubt, the fear of becoming embroiled in a conflict with the US is one source of the inhibition.

Past experience indicates that there are two basic reasons for Soviet intervention in another country: either because the Russians believe that their security, which includes their hold over satellite states, is being threatened, or because they think that the 'objective' conditions are right for setting up a regime which will be obedient to Moscow. 'Security' was the justification for Russian attempts to browbeat the Finns in 1958 and 1961, a situation the Finns handled by bending with the wind without breaking their fundamental stance of sturdy independence. Supporting a threatened regime against 'plots' fomented from without has been elevated to a principle of policy with the Brezhnev Doctrine of 1968, and was the excuse for the invasion of Afghanistan.

The threat of Russian intervention in a non-communist society is related to the domestic stability and health of the body politic. Up to the late 1970s Western Europe and Japan appeared to be both economically secure and politically stable. There were difficulties and tensions, of course, but they were contained within the democratic parameters of the state, and the general consensus began to extend even to some of the European communist parties and brought about the phenomenon of Euro-communism which put the Russians in a quandary. Since then the world has been plunged into the worst depression for fifty years, which is threatening to tear apart the social and political fabric of the industrialized countries. The danger has been contained so far, but the volatility of the electorate in some countries and, possibly more significant still, its disenchantment with the established parties, expressed through very high abstention rates in elections, is a warning of a deep-seated *malaise*. The mushroom-like growth of new parties and movements is another warning of potential fragility. Most disturbing of all is the effect of economic policies dictated by a rigid doctrine of monetarism and ruthless competition, which sharpen class antagonisms, create mass unemployment, and divide society into the successful well-to-do and the frustrated and embittered poor. There is plenty of material here for the Soviet Union to tamper with if it wants to undermine Western societies.

These may, of course, be passing phenomena. An economic recovery may be just round the corner, and even the most reactionary governments are eventually replaced in democratic societies. However, discussions of security often focus exclusively on the military threat and overlook the at least equally important threat which stems from social and political instability, which the Soviet Union has tried to exploit in the past. This aspect of security is not necessarily furthered by military preparations. On the contrary, they may be a diversion from more important social tasks, draining scarce resources into unproductive channels. Governments are also tempted to stress the threat from without in order to divert attention from the ills at home.

Security policy is not, therefore, confined to the defence of frontiers and, if the broader view is taken, it is likely that the purely military dimension will be seen as of limited importance – a hangover from the past rather than the answer to the problems of today.

A basic security policy seeks to ensure that the Soviet Union would not be tempted to take advantage of the exposed position of Europe and Japan to force them, through direct or indirect military pressure, to adopt a pro-Soviet position. It is equally intended that such a policy should not be seen as provocative by the Russians. The task is to provide security for both the Soviet Union and its Western neighbours.

There would be two elements in this approach. One would be based on existing conditions and the other would be an attempt to promote the relaxation of tensions and to reduce the importance of the military content of national security policy.

The basic structure of the existing alliances would be retained and their geographical limitations strictly observed. The integrated organization of the Atlantic Alliance would be modified to reduce the element of American domination. United States forces in Europe might be separated, so that there would be two distinct military organizations, one American and one European, existing side by side and acting in close liaison, but without a SACEUR who is American. Instead, the European partners might have their own SACEUR.

In spite of such changes, an American presence should be retained in Europe and Japan for all the reasons that have been advanced throughout this book. Moreover, the situation in Berlin requires it, as the United States, alongside the other three wartime allies, has a residual right to be in that city until a permanent solution to its status can be found. Attempts to squeeze out the Western allies have failed so far largely because of the presence of token forces in West Berlin. By themselves these troops could not offer serious resistance to a determined attack from the German Democratic Republic and the Soviet Union. However, the incalculable consequences of such a move have encouraged the Russians to make sure that their policies would not end in an armed confrontation.

Similar reasoning might apply to the presence of American forces elsewhere in Western Europe, but it does not seem necessary to maintain such large numbers. Half, or less than half the present establishment of some 250,000 men would surely be adequate to serve a similar purpose, especially if some units were stationed close to the borders of the Warsaw Pact. Some provision would have to be made for rapid reinforcement in an emergency. However, the deployment and capabilities of American and allied forces should be as unambiguously defensive as possible. They should not be able to launch a major attack on the Warsaw Pact, but should make sure that if the other side were so foolish as to launch an attack — or only a probe — westwards, it would come immediately face to face with American troops.

In East Asia a small number of American troops close to the Demilitarized Zone in Korea, as at present, and a small number of manned naval and air bases on the Japanese islands would serve the same purpose of signalling immediate American involvement in an armed confrontation and a strictly defensive strategy. Substantial force reductions in Europe and Asia would meet the American quest for economies, and make more palatable the loss of predominance in the alliances.

The application of this approach to nuclear armament is more difficult. The nuclear balance is so much a part of the superpower system that to tamper with it might create such a sense of insecurity on one side or the other that mutual restraint would break down in a crisis.

Moreover, the reduction of American conventional forces in Europe and East Asia is made possible because of the impact of nuclear deterrence. Nevertheless, a reduction of the nuclear armouries on both sides is imperative in the face of the growing tendency to think of these weapons in terms of the ability to fight and win a war.

The objective would be to reduce the American nuclear guarantee to an essentially off-shore force in both Europe and East Asia on the assumption that the physical presence of even a small number of American troops in both regions would guarantee the risk of nuclear confrontation. The existence of independent British and French nuclear forces presents rather different problems. Their credibility must remain in doubt, as a decision to use them in conflict would signal the intention to commit national suicide. On the other hand, they reinforce Russian caution because of the incalculable effect of their use on the American deterrent force.

A very strong case can be made for the abandonment of small national nuclear deterrents,[6] and in Britain it may not be difficult to gain general public support for such a policy. This does not appear to be so in France, and the strong likelihood that it would be left as the only West European state which possesses nuclear weapons strengthens the inertia of British governments against following so radical a policy as unilateral nuclear disarmament. A step in the right direction would be if British and French nuclear armament were reduced to a small submarine-based second-strike capability. In East Asia, Japan is to some extent inured against the temptation to go nuclear by its own 'allergy' and declared policy. The existence of a small and increasingly invulnerable Chinese nuclear deterrent also acts as a restraint on Soviet policy.

Everyone agrees that nuclear armaments have increased, are increasing, and ought to be diminished, but the record of attempts to achieve reductions is most discouraging. It points not only to the enormous vested interests behind these weapons, but also to deep-rooted psychological blocks in the way of reducing reliance on military force for security. The aim of a basic security policy would be to create a climate of opinion on both sides of the East-West divide, which is more receptive to attempts to break out of the spiralling arms race.

There are two methods of encouraging this process and they could be applied simultaneously. The first concentrates on confidence-building measures. The present may be a good time to revive the idea of Graduated and Reciprocated Initiatives in Tension-Reduction (GRIT), first advanced by the American psychologist Charles Osgood in the early

1960s.[7] The argument for GRIT is that traditional disarmament and arms-control negotiations require a prior commitment from both parties before either can act. Hence, the freedom of action of each is greatly restricted. Under GRIT, one party proposes to undertake a series of unilateral initiatives, inviting the other to respond. To be effective, the initiatives should be carried out according to a fixed timetable, regardless of whether the other side commits itself to reciprocate and regardless of crises which might develop during the period. Certain basic capabilities should be retained in the early stages of the process. It may gather momentum or slow down and come to a halt, all depending on whether the opponent enters into the spirit of the exercise or makes merely token responses or no response at all.

Although Osgood's proposal had the superpowers in mind, a similar approach could be applied to the relations between the lesser Western powers and the Soviet Union, particularly as it is as much the intention to create a favourable psychological climate as to achieve substantial progress in disarmament. Other confidence-building measures might include the signing of non-aggression treaties and other declaratory statements whose principal purpose would be to create a climate of good will. More practical steps would be mutual verification of arms control and disarmament measures, the exchange of missions to be posted at the headquarters of rival alliances with the object of mutual information about military manoeuvres and deployment and to serve as a channel of communication at times of tension. Another example would be the joint study and development of arms-control techniques and methods of inspection.

The second method of furthering the relaxation of tensions and reducing the importance of the military factor in relations with the Soviet Union is to develop defensive strategies. This idea has received some attention in recent years,[8] partly because of the apparent failure to make substantial progress in the more traditional approaches to international security through disarmament, arms control, and the establishment of international organizations to keep the peace. Defensive strategies can take a variety of forms, including a mixture of frontier defence, defence in depth, training for guerrilla action against an occupying power, and civilian defence with a predominant emphasis on non-violent resistance. A defensive strategy reformulates the question: 'What do we need to ensure our security?' to become: 'How can we provide for our security in ways which do *not* threaten the security of other states?'. To think in such terms would be to link the concept of national defence to the concept of international security.[9]

The development of a particular mix of defensive measures is bound to vary with the circumstances of the state. The security problems of Western Europe are not identical to those of Japan. Given its geographical environment and the remarkable homogeneity and social discipline of its population, Japan is in an excellent position to develop such an inoffensive strategy which is, indeed, required by its constitution. Among the states of Western Europe, a defensive strategy which might be suitable for Britain[10] would not necessarily be suitable for the Federal Republic of Germany[11] or France. A country which pursues such a strategy is like a hedgehog. Inoffensive creature that it is, it rolls itself into a tight ball and presents a most unpalatable prospect to any would-be attacker.

The policies described so far have the objective of providing for national security without appearing to threaten one's neighbours. Thus, it is hoped to lower, if not to eliminate entirely, the most important barrier to the creation of mutual trust. But this would not be enough without the simultaneous and vigorous pursuit of more positive policies.

The idea behind such initiatives would be to establish the four states as intermediaries and mediators between the rival superpowers and, in a wider sense, to exercise a constructive influence in world affairs. This would require the deliberate fostering of economic, technological and cultural relations with both superpowers and between them. One would have to accept an asymmetry in the openness of the two types of society, but instead of curtailing intercourse between the Soviet Union and the West on a childish tit-for-tat basis, every effort should be made to encourage a more open approach by the Soviet Union through example and persuasion. Experience has shown that this is not impossible, as when President Nixon appeared on Soviet television on 28 May 1972, and, more recently, when the *Guardian* in an imaginative gesture sent fifteen of its feature writers to Russia in an attempt to give its readers a comprehensive impression of Soviet society.[12]

The second strand in the positive approach would be the promotion of internationalism in world affairs through the agencies of the United Nations and other international organizations. It would include support for multilateral economic assistance and development projects, the establishment of international regimes in various regions and in specific fields of human enterprise, on the lines of those already existing, such as the Antarctic Treaty of 1959, the Peaceful Uses of Outer Space Treaty of 1967, and the agreements concerning the uses of the seabed. Most important would be the strengthening of international machinery for keeping the peace.

Armed clashes will continue to be a feature of world politics, especially in the revolutionary ferment of the Third World. International intervention under the auspices of the United Nations does not necessarily lead to a resolution of conflicts, as witness the many unfinished wars in the world, but it can have a restraining influence on the parties by making their quarrels the world's business. The absence of such intervention might have a more deleterious effect in the long term.

The clash between Argentina and Britain over the Falkland Islands in the spring of 1982 is a case in point. The sense of outrage at Argentina's aggression and the strongly felt need for a speedy British reaction made it particularly difficult to resort to protracted negotiations under UN auspices. The short-term consequence of the armed confrontation was a clear British victory, but the long-term consequence is an arms race in the South Atlantic, ruinous to Argentina's already shaky economy and a drain on British resources which, it is generally agreed, cannot be sustained indefinitely. Sooner or later the two parties must come to a settlement, and a solution acceptable to both may well include an element of internationalization.

Much should therefore be done to improve the machinery for the control of crises and conflicts at the disposal of the United Nations. The West European states and Japan could play an important part in the process by contributing their experience and resources. The Federal Republic of Germany and Japan, in particular, are in the position to make a special contribution on account of their recent history and postwar orientation.

The third strand of positive action would consist of measures to promote joint ventures with Third World countries which are aimed at assisting their economic development and social stability. We have noted in Chapter 5 that this is a complex problem as the interests of the industrialized states conflict as well as coincide. Governments would have to co-operate with international companies, and a balance struck between the immediate interest of the Western states in ensuring supplies of raw materials and markets for their products and the longer-term interest of building up the economic strength of the developing countries. Such policies would be in line with the recommendations of the Brandt Report.[13] The objective would be to assist Third World countries in maintaining their independence from superpower domination. To promote peaceful change in Asia, Africa and Latin America, the four states should also resist the temptation of trying to gain markets, influence and favour through the sale of arms.

European-Japanese Co-operation as a Positive Element in World Politics

The last question that has to be considered is to what extent Europe and Japan can be expected to coordinate their policies in pursuit of the objectives described above. This is a matter both of shared interests and the machinery through which they can be expressed. Since most of this book has been devoted to a discussion of interests and policies, I shall first consider ways and means before returning in the concluding pages to a final assessment of the problem of developing common policies.

The form of political co-operation between the major European states and Japan cannot be served by institutionalizing trilateralism and making it official, for West Europe and Japan must consult and coordinate among themselves before entering into a dialogue with the United States. Within the Atlantic Alliance it is widely accepted that unless the West European states speak with one voice, they cannot hope to carry much weight in the deliberations of Washington, where the budget of the Pentagon alone is equal to the national budget of one of the smaller allies. All the more reason, then, for the West European states and Japan to speak with one voice when it comes to discussing global affairs with the United States.

Moreover, continuing and developing the pattern of trilateralism would be contrary to the development of a mediating role. It would be a move in the opposite direction: the expansion of two American-dominated alliances into a larger alliance. The Russians would rightly see in this a ganging up against themselves. On the other hand, the same reasoning that applies to a Euro-Japanese dialogue with the US applies to the dialogue with the Soviet Union. Joint Euro-Japanese approaches to the Russians would be more effective than those made by individual states.

In considering the structures within which West European and Japanese collaboration could be developed, there are several models from which to choose. One, the alliance model, has to be ruled out from the start for four reasons. First, there is the simple fact of geography. Secondly, constitutional and political constraints within Japan make it impossible and undesirable. Thirdly, we are far from the kind of unity in Western Europe which would make the concept of a European-Japanese 'alliance' a feasible proposition. Lastly, an alliance would be contrary to the idea of getting away from the purely confrontational aspect of relations with the Soviet Union.

Therefore, the association would have to take the form of some sort of procedures for consultation. It could be an institutionalized encounter between foreign ministers, interspersed with less frequent summit meetings. This would merely be an extension of the current bilateral meetings between Japan and the various European states. Alternatively, the consultation could follow the UN caucus model, making it a special feature at the annual meetings of the General Assembly. This would mean that further pressures on the already crowded schedules of busy foreign ministers could be avoided since they normally attend the General Assembly in the autumn. A different and more highly structured form of consultation would be the establishment of a small secretariat, similar to the Commonwealth or ASEAN secretariats, which would handle the machinery of consultation all the year round.

The great advantage of this last arrangement would be a more thorough and wide-ranging association than could be provided by very short periodic meetings of senior ministers. Such a secretariat would handle political, economic and cultural business of common concern at lower levels on a day-to-day basis, and develop a thickening web of contacts between Europe and Japan. One further benefit would be the opportunity for European and Japanese officials to become more familiar with each other's outlook and methods of work. Cultural and linguistic barriers are still serious impediments to achieving the kind of easy intercourse that exists between Europeans and Americans.

In the economic field the Europeans already have machinery which enables them to speak with one voice, and it might be possible to relate it to a structure of Euro-Japanese consultation. It would be different in the political field, where each state jealously guards its liberty. It is likely, therefore, that within a developing European-Japanese dialogue, Japan will find itself working more closely at the beginning with one of the West European states than with the others.

The obvious candidate for this role would be the Federal Republic of Germany. The two countries have a great deal in common. Their historical background has interesting parallels, they have both broken with their militaristic past, and each has achieved phenomenal economic success in spite of very limited natural resources.[14] Furthermore, their relationship in recent years has been least affected by the economic friction which has roused such ill-feeling towards Japan in France and Britain.

Japan and the Federal Republic of Germany are the most important friends of the United States, and have a particular interest in maintaining a security relationship with it, but the two countries are also likely to seek a more independent role because of their growing influence in the world. Both have compelling reasons for creating zones of stability and peace within their regions, which would serve both to inhibit Soviet expansion and to give them greater freedom from the constraints of American policy. Their geographical location makes them natural cores of such zones. German leadership in the pursuit of détente in Europe and Japanese interest in an association of Pacific states could be pointers towards such a development.

Progress in formulating common European and Japanese positions and policies over relations with the United States, the Soviet Union and the Third World is bound to be uneven. The Federal Republic and Japan may have the greatest affinity in outlook because of certain basic similarities in their national security problems, but a wider West European-Japanese coordination would be much more difficult to achieve for two reasons. Each of the four states has particular preoccupations and concerns which stand in the way of harmonization, and which they are not easily persuaded to give up for the sake of a unified approach to some issue or another. This characteristic has already been discussed at length in various parts of the book and need not be stressed here. The second reason is to be found in the very different problems facing the two regions.

The division of Germany and its consequences are the key factors of East-West relations in Europe. The existence of two alliances, each led by a superpower and in direct confrontation at the centre of the continent, is another factor. The link between the conventional and theatre nuclear balances in Europe and the central strategic balance between the United States and Russia is a third factor. Finally, the extraordinarily difficult and complex Soviet-East European relationship adds a fourth element to the European situation.

Quite different factors are to be found in East Asia. No West European state has a territorial dispute with the Soviet Union such as the one that exists between Japan and Russia over the Northern Territories. East Asia has only a superficial bipolar confrontation, and with the emergence of China is set to move into a triangular power structure. China cannot hope to compete militarily with either the Soviet Union or the United States within this century, but its size and regional importance enable it to play an independent role, such as France under de Gaulle aspired to but never fully achieved. The future of the region may be dominated by competition between the United States and China over the friendship of Japan; not against each other but for different ends: the United States seeking to enlist Japan in its world-wide anti-

Soviet front while China tries to draw Japan into close association to form a regional bloc which will bar the way to the Soviet Union, but is not tied to America's global policies. Japan's function in each partnership would be to provide capital, high technology and human skill, with military power playing a subordinate role, though probably more important than it is at present.

For these reasons alone, it would appear that a Euro-Japanese bloc is well outside the realm of practical politics. Furthermore, the argument against the formation of blocs, which has been advanced in this book, would make such a development undesirable. The articulation of coordinated or joint West European and Japanese policies over specific issues is a much more likely development, and we have already seen some examples of this. However, a precondition of more effective and sustained collaboration must be the improvement of bilateral relations.

So far, at least, Japan has taken the lead in the coordination of policies by attendance at the meeting of EEC foreign ministers in Luxembourg in April 1980, during Ōhira's and Suzuki's visits to Europe in May 1980 and June 1981, by expressing the wish to participate in contingency planning over Poland, and by instituting regular visits by officials to NATO Headquarters in Brussels. It is easy to see why this should have been so. Japan is emerging from a period of semi-isolation when its foreign and security policies were dominated by its close association with the United States. The leaders of Western Europe have not been accustomed to take Japan into account when dealing with the United States, the Soviet Union or the Third World. Their overriding concern has been with the trans-Atlantic relationship and with their security against the Soviet Union. Japan was just a tiresome and threatening economic problem. Ironically, it is American pressure on the European and Japanese allies to do more for the *common* defence which is not only bringing Japan out into the open, but is establishing the basis for European and Japanese co-operation.

However much the allies share the American concern over the current trend of Soviet policy, they do not share the basic American perception of the Soviet Union. They are not superpowers, and their geographical location brings them into more intimate contact with the Russians. Europeans and Japanese, therefore, have more in common with each other in this respect than with the Americans.

They also have a common interest in not wanting the Third World to be carved up between the superpowers. Their relations with many of the countries in those regions are founded on an economic interdependence, especially in so far as oil and other sources of energy are concerned, which does not apply in the same degree to American or Soviet relations with the Third World. Those two powers are more concerned with the place of the Third World in the balance of power between themselves, and they look upon it largely, if not exclusively, in terms of advantage and disadvantage against the rival. Hence the American tendency to bolster authoritarian and corrupt regimes against the better judgement of their major European allies. The Japanese do not appear to be as bothered by such considerations, but they are distinctly bothered by American pressures against economic relations with countries in the 'enemy' camp.

Over issues relating to the Soviet Union and the Third World, West Europeans and Japanese share common interests and could, without too much difficulty, present a united front in Washington. The Europeans are beginning to do this, and various developments, such as the establishment of the Eurogroup in NATO and the European peace initiative in the Middle East, are indicative of the trend. To include Japan in joint action over matters of mutual interest would further strengthen their bargaining power. There is no reason why this kind of collaboration could not also be established for dealings with the Soviet Union. A typical example is the multilateral interest in the supply of natural gas from Russia to Western Europe, in which Japanese industry is also involved.

I have argued that the pursuit of defensive strategies and constructive 'internationalist' policies is the best way forward for Japan and the major states of Western Europe. Such policies would be designed to halt the tendency towards global confrontation, and would avoid the dangers of simply creating more power blocs, perpetuating the threat of periodic adjustments of the balance of power through trials of armed strength.

The policies would also diminish the ideological content of relationships among the major powers. International relations would be conducted on the principle of dealing with specific issues and interests, always looking for their peaceful adjustment. Interstate relations should be managed in a businesslike manner and not in terms of abstract and irreconcilable principles. This would be in contrast to the high-flown rhetoric in which the superpowers clothe their policies, and which serve to inflame public opinion against each other.

Another major objective would be a reduction of the importance of military power in interstate relations through multilateral negotiations, unilateral initiatives, and defensive postures. In the past the concepts of national defence and international peace have usually been regarded as mutually exclusive, in the sense that the search for national security tended to ignore the security of other countries. Defensive strategies should be sufficiently impressive and determined to act as a deterrent against a would-be aggressor, but they should also reassure other states by dispensing with those organizational structures and weapons systems which would enable one to attack and occupy their territories.

The four states of this study have the experience, the resources, and the interests to take such initiatives in concert. There are, of course, geographical, historical and cultural factors, as well as some conflicting interests, which will restrain progress towards concerted action. But there have been recent indications of a move in this direction. Even if there had been so such indications, collaboration is becoming imperative if we want to develop new concepts for the management of international relations in which war and the threat of war become increasingly irrelevant as instruments of policy.

Notes

1. *Strategic Survey 1981-1982* (London, International Institute for Strategic Studies, Spring 1982), pp. 104, 106-7.
2. For prognostications of such an event see, for example, Sir John Hackett *et al., The Third World War: A Future History* (London, Book Club Associates, by arrangement with Sidgwick & Jackson, 1978). Such scenarios often tell us more about the mentality of those who dream them up and the psychological climate of the time, than about what is likely to happen. None the less and rather frighteningly, if taken seriously by those responsible for the affairs of state, they have the potential of a self-fulfilling prophecy. I.F. Clarke's *Voices Prophesying War, 1763-1984* (London, OUP, 1966) is a fascinating and illuminating study of the literature which purports to describe future wars.
3. George Orwell, *Nineteen Eighty-four* (Harmondsworth, Middlesex, Penguin Books in association with Secker & Warburg, 1971), pp. 6, 14, 29-31, 125, 146-8, 150-61.
4. Jean-Jacques Servan-Schreiber, *Le Défi américain* (Paris, Denoël, 1967). Tranlsated by Ronald Steel in *The American Challenge* (London, Hamish Hamilton, 1968).
5. For an early discussion of the theory and practice of non-alignment, see John W. Burton, *International Relations: A General Theory* (London, Cambridge University Press, 1965).
6. See, for example, Michael Carver, *A Policy for Peace* (London, Faber & Faber, 1982).
7. Charles E. Osgood, *An Alternative to War or Surrender* (Urbana, Ill., University of Illinois Press, 1962), especially pp. 102-3, 111.
8. For examples of defensive strategies practised by the neutral states of Europe, see Adam Roberts, *Nations in Arms: The Theory and Practice of Territorial Defence* (London, Chatto & Windus for the International Institute for Strategic Studies, 1976). The same author has edited a symposium on the practice of non-violent resistance, *The Strategy of Civilian Defence: Non-Violent*

Resistance to Aggression (London, Faber & Faber, 1967). For an excellent study of the implications of a policy of non-violence, see Leroy H. Pelton, *The Psychology of Nonviolence* (New York, Pergamon Press, 1974).

9. Wolf Mendl, 'Reducing Distrust and Tensions between Nations through Defensive Strategies', in 'Peace and Security in a Changing World', *Proceedings of the Twenty-Seventh Pugwash Conference on Science and World Affairs*, Munich, 24-29 August 1977 (published in 1978), pp. 353-6.

10. See *Defence Without the Bomb*, the Report of the Alternative Defence Commission set up by the Lansbury House Trust Fund (London, Taylor & Francis Ltd, 1983).

11. An ingenious proposal for a West German defensive strategy is to be found in Horst Afheldt, *Verteidigung und Frieden: Politik mit Militärischen Mitteln* (München, Carl Hanser Verlag, 1976), especially the second part of the book from p. 209 onwards. See also Carl Friedrich von Weizsäcker (ed.), *Kriegsfolgen und Kriegsverhütung* (München, Carl Hanser Verlag, 1971).

12. *Guardian*, 11-16 April 1983.

13. *North-South: A Programme for Survival* (Report of the Independent Commission on Development Issues, Chairman: Willy Brandt, London, Pan, 1980).

14. Arnulf Baring und Masamori Sase (eds), *Zwei Zaghafte Riesen? Deutschland und Japan seit 1945* (Stuttgart, Belser Verlag, 1977).

GLOSSARY

ABM	Anti-ballistic Missile(s)
ANF	Atlantic Nuclear Force
ANZUS	Pacific Defence Pact signed in 1951 between Australia, New Zealand and USA
ASEAN	Association of South-east Asian Nations
ASW	Anti-submarine Warfare
AWACS	Airborne Warning and Control System
BAM	Baikal-Amur Railway
CND	Campaign for Nuclear Disarmament
COMECON	Council for Mutual Economic Assistance
DAC	Development Assistance Committee (OECD)
EDC	European Defence Community
EEC	European Economic Community (Common Market)
EEZ	Exclusive Economic Zone
EFTA	European Free Trade Association
GRIT	Graduated and Reciprocated Initiatives in Tension-reduction
ICBM	Intercontinental Ballistic Missile(s)
INF	Intermediate-range Nuclear Forces
IRBM	Intermediate-range Ballistic Missile(s)
LDCs	Least Developed Countries
LRTNF	Long-range Theatre Nuclear Force(s)
MLF	Multilateral Force
NICs	Newly Industrialized Countries
NPT	Non-proliferation Treaty
ODA	Official Development Assistance
OECD	Organization for Economic Co-operation and Development
OPEC	Organization of Petroleum-exporting Countries
SACEUR	Supreme Allied Commander Europe
SALT	Strategic Arms Limitation Talks
SCAP	Supreme Commander Allied Powers
SDF	Self-defence Forces
SLBM	Submarine-launched Ballistic Missile(s)
SSBN	Ballistic-missile Nuclear Submarine(s)

Glossary

START	Strategic Arms Reduction Talks
TNF	Theatre Nuclear Force(s)
WEU	Western European Union
ZOPFAN	Zone of Peace, Freedom and Neutrality

APPENDIX I: THE NORTH ATLANTIC TREATY, WASHINGTON DC, 4 APRIL 1949*

The Parties to this Treaty reaffirm their faith in the purposes and principles of the Charter of the United Nations and their desire to live in peace with all peoples and all Governments.

They are determined to safeguard the freedom, common heritage and civilization of their peoples, founded on the principles of democracy, individual liberty and the rule of law.

They seek to promote stability and well-being in the North Atlantic area.

They are resolved to unite their efforts for collective defence and for the preservation of peace and security.

They therefore agree to this North Atlantic Treaty:

ARTICLE I

The Parties undertake, as set forth in the Charter of the United Nations, to settle any international dispute in which they may be involved by peaceful means in such a manner that international peace and security and justice are not endangered, and to refrain in their international relations from the threat or use of force in any manner inconsistent with the purposes of the United Nations.

ARTICLE 2

The Parties will contribute toward the further development of peaceful and friendly international relations by strengthening their free institutions, by bringing about a better understanding of the principles upon which these institutions are founded, and by promoting conditions of stability and well-being. They will seek to eliminate conflict in their international economic policies and will encourage economic collaboration between any or all of them.

---

*The Treaty came into force on 24 August 1949, after the deposition of the ratifications of all signatory states.

Appendix I

ARTICLE 3

In order more effectively to achieve the objectives of this Treaty, the Parties, separately and jointly, by means of continuous and effective self-help and mutual aid, will maintain and develop their individual and collective capacity to resist armed attack.

ARTICLE 4

The Parties will consult together whenever, in the opinion of any of them, the territorial integrity, political independence or security of any of the Parties is threatened.

ARTICLE 5

The Parties agree that an armed attack against one or more of them in Europe or North America shall be considered an attack against them all, and consequently they agree that, if such an armed attack occurs, each of them, in exercise of the right of individual or collective self-defence recognized by Article 51 of the Charter of the United Nations, will assist the Party or Parties so attacked by taking forthwith, individually, and in concert with the other Parties, such action as it deems necessary, including the use of armed force, to restore and maintain the security of the North Atlantic area.

Any such armed attack and all measures taken as a result thereof shall immediately be reported to the Security Council. Such measures shall be terminated when the Security Council has taken the measures necessary to restore and maintain international peace and security.

ARTICLE 6*

For the purpose of Article 5, an armed attack on one or more of the Parties is deemed to include an armed attack
— on the territory of any of the Parties in Europe or North America, on the Algerian Departments of France,** on the territory of

---

*As amended by Article 2 of the Protocol to the North Atlantic Treaty on the accession of Greece and Turkey.
**On 16 January 1963 the French Representative made a statement to the North Atlantic Council on the effects of the independence of Algeria on certain aspects of the North Atlantic Treaty. The Council noted that insofar as the former Algerian Departments of France were concerned the relevant clauses of this Treaty had become inapplicable as from 3 July 1962.

Turkey or on the islands under the jurisdiction of any of the Parties in the North Atlantic area north of the Tropic of Cancer;
— on the forces, vessels, or aircraft of any of the Parties, when in or over these territories or any area in Europe in which occupation forces of any of the Parties were stationed on the date when the Treaty entered into force or the Mediterranean Sea or the North Atlantic area north of the Tropic of Cancer.

ARTICLE 7

This Treaty does not effect, and shall not be interpreted as affecting, in any way the rights and obligations under the Charter of the Parties which are members of the United Nations, or the primary responsibility of the Security Council for the maintenance of international peace and security.

ARTICLE 8

Each Party declares that none of the international engagements now in force between it and any other of the Parties or any third State is in conflict with the provisions of this Treaty, and undertakes not to enter into any international engagement in conflict with this Treaty.

ARTICLE 9

The Parties hereby establish a Council, on which each of them shall be represented to consider matters concerning the implementation of this Treaty. The Council shall be so organized as to be able to meet promptly at any time. The Council shall set up such subsidiary bodies as may be necessary; in particular it shall establish immediately a defence committee which shall recommend measures for the implementation of Articles 3 and 5.

ARTICLE 10

The Parties may, by unanimous agreement, invite any other European State in a position to further the principles of this Treaty and to contribute to the security of the North Atlantic area to accede to this Treaty. Any State so invited may become a party to the Treaty by depositing its instrument of accession with the Government of the United States of America. The Government of the United States of America will inform each of the Parties of the deposit of each such instrument of accession.

ARTICLE 11

This Treaty shall be ratified and its provisions carried out by the Parties in accordance with their respective constitutional processes. The instruments of ratification shall be deposited as soon as possible with the Government of the United States of America, which will notify all the other signatories of each deposit. The Treaty shall enter into force between the States which have ratified it as soon as the ratification of the majority of the signatories, including the ratifications of Belgium, Canada, France, Luxembourg, the Netherlands, the United Kingdom and the United States, have been deposited and shall come into effect with respect to other States on the date of the deposit of their ratifications.

ARTICLE 12

After the Treaty has been in force for ten years, or at any time thereafter, the Parties shall, if any of them so requests, consult together for the purpose of reviewing the Treaty, having regard for the factors then affecting peace and security in the North Atlantic area including the development of universal as well as regional arrangements under the Charter of the United Nations for the maintenance of international peace and security.

ARTICLE 13

After the Treaty has been in force for twenty years, any Party may cease to be a Party one year after its notice of denunciation has been given to the Government of the United States of America, which will inform the Governments of the other Parties of the deposit of each notice of denunciation.

ARTICLE 14

This Treaty, of which the English and French texts are equally authentic, shall be deposited in the archives of the Government of the United States of America. Duly certified copies will be transmitted by that Government to the Governments of the other signatories.

Source: *NATO Handbook* (Brussels, NATO Information Service, March 1982), pp. 13-16.

APPENDIX II: TREATY OF MUTUAL COOPERATION AND SECURITY BETWEEN THE UNITED STATES OF AMERICA AND JAPAN, WASHINGTON DC, 19 JANUARY 1960

The United States of America and Japan,
Desiring to strengthen the bonds of peace and friendship traditionally existing between them, and to uphold the principles of democracy, individual liberty, and the rule of law,
Desiring further to encourage closer economic cooperation between them and to promote conditions of economic stability and well-being in their countries,
Reaffirming their faith in the purposes and principles of the Charter of the United Nations, and their desire to live in peace with all peoples and all governments,
Recognizing that they have the inherent right of individual or collective self-defense as affirmed in the Charter of the United Nations,
Considering that they have a common concern in the maintenance of international peace and security in the Far East,
Having resolved to conclude a treaty of mutual cooperation and security,
Therefore agree as follows:

ARTICLE I

The Parties undertake, as set forth in the Charter of the United Nations, to settle any international disputes in which they may be involved by peaceful means in such a manner that international peace and security and justice are not endangered and to refrain in their international relations from the threat or use of force against the territorial integrity or political independence of any state, or in any other manner inconsistent with the purposes of the United Nations.

The Parties will endeavor in concert with other peace-loving countries to strengthen the United Nations so that its mission of maintaining international peace and security may be discharged more effectively.

ARTICLE II

The Parties will contribute toward the further development of peaceful and friendly international relations by strengthening their free institutions, by bringing about a better understanding of the principles upon which these institutions are founded, and by promoting conditions of stability and well being. They will seek to eliminate conflict in their international economic policies and will encourage economic collaboration between them.

ARTICLE III

The Parties, individually and in cooperation with each other, by means of continuous and effective self-help and mutual aid will maintain and develop, subject to their constitutional provisions, their capacities to resist armed attack.

ARTICLE IV

The Parties will consult together from time to time regarding the implementation of this Treaty, and, at the request of either Party, whenever the security of Japan or international peace and security in the Far East is threatened.

ARTICLE V

Each Party recognizes that an armed attack against either Party in the territories under the administration of Japan would be dangerous to its own peace and safety and declares that it would act to meet the common danger in accordance with its constitutional provisions and processes.
Any such armed attack and all measures taken as a result thereof shall be immediately reported to the Security Council of the United Nations in accordance with the provisions of Article 51 of the Charter. Such measures shall be terminated when the Security Council has taken the measures necessary to restore and maintain international peace and security.

ARTICLE VI

For the purpose of contributing to the security of Japan and the maintenance of international peace and security in the Far East, The United States of America is granted the use by its land, air and naval forces of facilities and areas in Japan.

The use of these facilities and areas as well as the status of United States armed forces in Japan shall be governed by a separate agreement, replacing the Administrative Agreement under Article III of the Security Treaty between the United States of America and Japan, signed at Tokyo on February 28, 1952, as amended, and by such other arrangements as may be agreed upon.

ARTICLE VII

This Treaty does not affect and shall not be interpreted as affecting in any way the rights and obligations of the Parties under the Charter of the United Nations or the responsibility of the United Nations for the maintenance of international peace and security.

ARTICLE VIII

This Treaty shall be ratified by the United States of America and Japan in accordance with their respective constitutional processes and will enter into force on the date on which the instruments of ratification thereof have been exchanged by them in Tokyo.

ARTICLE IX

The Security Treaty between the United States of America and Japan signed at the city of San Francisco on September 8, 1951, shall expire upon the entering into force of this Treaty.

ARTICLE X

This Treaty shall remain in force until in the opinion of the Governments of the United States of America and Japan there shall have come into force such United Nations arrangements as will satisfactorily provide for the maintenance of international peace and security in the Japan area.

However, after the Treaty has been in force for ten years, either Party may give notice to the other Party of its intention to terminate the Treaty, in which case the Treaty shall terminate one year after such

Appendix II

notice has been given.

Source: *U.S. Department of State Bulletin*, vol. XLII, no. 1076, 8 February 1960, pp. 184-5.

INDEX

Acheson, Dean 86, 111n5
Aden 114
Adenauer, Konrad 59-60, 63
Afghanistan 52, 76, 100, 130-2, 135, 146; EEC proposals on 109; Soviet invasion 19, 28, 57, 79-80, 106, 134, 144, 152
Afro-Asian non-aligned movement 9
airborne warning and control system (AWACS) 73
Algeria 33, 57, 129; war in 43, 114
Allied Control Council (Germany) 45
Allied Council for Japan 45
Angola 15, 97, 130-1, 136, 144
Antarctic Treaty (1959) 157
Anti-Ballistic Missile (ABM) Deployment Agreement (1972) 14
Anzus Pact (1951) 89
Arbenz Guzmán, Jacopo 19
Argentina 64, 102; and nuclear energy 18; war with Britain 50, 144, 158
Association of South-east Asian Nations (ASEAN) 21, 66, 79, 110, 124, 144, 150; secretariat 160; *see also* European Economic Community
Atlantic Alliance 21-2, 36, 38, 49, 63, 78, 107, 159; admission of German Federal Republic 59; and Falklands war 50; commitment to annual increase in expenditure 92-3; Eurogroup 163; forces in Europe 71-4; integrated organization 56, 153-4; Japan's relations with 143-4, 162; North Atlantic Treaty 57-8, 81n4, 168-71; sense of crisis 51; *see also* Gaulle, Charles de
Atlantic Nuclear Force (ANF) 60
'Atoms for Peace' 9
Australia 79, 118, 121-2, 141
Austria 94

Backfire Bomber 75, 78
Baikal-Amur Railway (BAM) 101, 105

Baluchis 131
Bandar-Khomeini, Japanese-Iranian petrochemical complex 115
Bangladesh 123
Beirut 80
Belgium 121
Berlin 44, 45-6, 85, 90, 107, 134; blockade 34, 86
Bevin, Ernest 87-8
Bolivia 121
Brandt Report 158
Brazil 11, 64, 143
Bretton Woods Agreement 7
Brezhnev, Leonid 70; Brezhnev Doctrine 152; *see also* Nixon, Richard M.
Britain 6; Campaign for Nuclear Disarmament (CND) 76; Empire 35, 150; Engineering Employers' Federation 136; European policy 35-6; food imports 122; Foreign Office 43; industrial raw materials 119-22, 138; international trade 125-6; Labour Party 58, 148-9; military policy 33-4, 42-3; nuclear armament 18, 38-41, 155; overseas aid and investment 122-4; relationship with US 36, 38-41, 58-9; sources of energy 116-19, 138; withdrawal from east of Suez 36, 67, 78; *see also* Argentina, Commonwealth, Falkland Islands
British Leyland 133, 137
Brunei 117-18
Brzezinski, Zbigniew 65, 75
Bulgaria 84, 100, 130
Burma 123

Cambodia 130, 135-6, 144
Campaign for Nuclear Disarmament 76, 92
Canada 118, 121-2, 141; and India's first nuclear explosion 18; and Standing Group in Washington 56
Carrington, Lord 109
Carter, Jimmy 75, 133; Administra-

Index

tion 64-6, 77
Central African Republic 114
Chad 49-50, 114
Chile 98, 121
China 46, 64, 121, 126, 129, 141, 143-4, 146, 161; ancient 12, 140; and Korea 86-7, 90; as military power 10, 18, 23, 155; permanent member of Security Council 10; relations with Soviet Union 9, 19, 74, 86-7, 130, 147; relations with United States 15, 88-9, 132, 139n9, 144; *see also* Japan
Churchill, Winston S. 87
Cold War 8-9, 11, 88-9
Cominform 84-5
Comintern 84
Common Market *see* European Economic Community
Commonwealth 35, 124; countries in South-east Asia 67, *see also* Malaya, Singapore; secretariat 160; zone of occupation in Japan 45
Congo-Brazzaville 130
Council for Mutual Economic Assistance (COMECON) 144
cruise-launched missiles 2, 60
Cuba 52, 129, 131-3, 143-4; missile crisis 9, 14, 70, 90, 145; troops abroad 96-7, 144
Czechoslovakia 19, 88, 131; Prague *coup* (1948) 84

defensive strategies 156-7
deterrence 13; *see also* Soviet Union, United States
Development Assistance Committee (DAC) 123
Dimona reactor 18
Dominican Republic 19
Dulles, John Foster 59, 145

Eden, Anthony 59
Egypt 19, 123-4; and Soviet Union 15, 130-2, 144; peace settlement with Israel 15, 23; *see also* Nasser, Gamal Abdul; Suez Canal
Eisenhower, Dwight D. 62-3; 'open skies' proposals 9, 89
El Salvador 19, 97, 109, 136
Engels, Friedrich 140
Enhanced Radiation Weapon (neutron bomb) 65-6

Ethiopia 97, 131, 144
Euro-communism 96, 152
European Defence Community (EDC) 59
European Economic Community (EEC) 8, 94, 122, 134, 143; and Japan 25-8, 125-6; and Siberian pipeline 103; initiative over Palestine 109; meeting of foreign ministers in Luxembourg (1980) 134-5, 162; meeting with ASEAN foreign ministers in Kuala Lumpur (1980) 135; proposals on Afghanistan 109; Soviet hostility towards 106
European Free Trade Association (EFTA) 94, 151

F-111 aircraft 36
Falkland Islands 50, 114, 158
Far Eastern Commission 45
Federal Republic of Germany: admission to Atlantic Alliance 59; and Non-Proliferation Treaty 48; and nuclear energy 18; arms exports 51; Basic Law 47-8, 54n24; change of government (1982) 10, 30n4, 92; food imports 122; industrial raw materials 119-22; international trade 125-6; Ostpolitik 60, 90; overseas aid and investment 122-4; relations with US 59-60; sources of energy 115-19; twenty-five-year agreement with Soviet Union (1978) 102; *see also* Schmidt, Helmut
Finland 85, 88, 93-5, 112n16, 152; Agreement of Friendship, Co-operation and Mutual Assistance with Soviet Union 106-7; 'Finlandization' 93-4
First World War 6, 44, 87
France 6-7, 18, 37, 92, 148; and Atlantic Alliance 38, 56, 81n2; Communist Party 38, 85, 91, 95, 112n18; Empire 150; food exports 122; German policy 37, 42, 91; industrial raw materials 119-22; international trade 125-6; military policy 33, 42-4; naval presence in Indian Ocean 78; nuclear armament 18, 41-2, 155; overseas aid and investment

122-4; policy towards Soviet Union 91; relations with US 60-1; sources of energy 115-19; *see also* Gaulle, Charles de; Giscard d'Estaing, Valéry
French Revolution 147

Gaulle, Charles de 9, 37-8, 41, 60-1, 81n2, 90-1, 96, 161; Europe from the Atlantic to the Urals 21, 38; Gaullism 148-9
Geneva 89
German Democratic Republic 131, 154
German Federal Republic *see* Federal Republic of Germany
Germany 6-7; currency reform in Western zones of occupation 86; occupation of 44-6
Ghana 121
Giscard d'Estaing, Valéry 109
Graduated and Reciprocated Initiatives in Tension-Reduction (GRIT) 155-6
Greece 57, 71, 121, 126
Greenland 121
Guardian 157
Guatemala 19
Guinea 121, 131
Gulf region 58, 64, 68, 79, 131, 146; states 66
Guyana 121

Hallstein Doctrine 91, 111-12n12
Heath, Edward 58
Helsinki accords 89, 107
Herter, Christian A. 62
HMS *Endurance* 50
Hokkaido 89, 108
Holy Alliance 98
Horn of Africa 15
Hungary 19, 84, 88, 131
Huntington, Samuel P. 47, 54n23

India 11, 64, 141, 143; first nuclear explosion 18
Indian Ocean 23, 35, 66-7, 78
Indochina 21, 33, 66-7, 129; Geneva conferences on 89; refugees 135; war (1946-54) 114
Indonesia 117-18, 121, 123, 130
Intermediate-range Nuclear Forces (INF) 2; in the Asian region 77-8
International Atomic Energy Agency 9
Iran 64, 100, 121, 131-2; hostage crisis 76, 134; revolution 19, 28, 124; war with Iraq 146
Iraq 131, 146
Ireland 121
Israel 15, 132, 144, 146; and nuclear energy 18; peace settlement with Egypt 15, 23; *see also* Beirut
Italy 59, 85, 95
Itō, Masayoshi 65

Jamaica 124
Japan 6-7, 25, 45, 53-4n21, 89; and Non-Proliferation Treaty 48; and nuclear armament 76, 82-3n24; and nuclear energy 18; arms exports 51; Communist Party 85, 111n3; economic co-operation with Soviet Union 104-5, 112n27; food imports 122, 138; industrial raw materials 119-22, 138; international trade 125-6; Korean policy 90; Liberal-Democratic Party 92; Machinery Exporters' Association 136; normalization of relations with Soviet Union 89; Northern Territories 74, 161; occupation of 45-6, 85-6; overseas aid and investment 122-5, 139n4; relations with China 25, 63-4, 90-1, 104-5, 140, 150; Self-Defence Forces (SDF) 47, 51, 74; sources of energy 115-19, 138; *see also* Association of South-east Asian Nations, Atlantic Alliance, European Economic Community, Treaty of Mutual Cooperation and Security between US and Japan
Johnson, Lyndon B. 56, 81n2; meeting with Kosygin in Glassboro 15

Kabinda 136-7
Kahn, Herman 17, 31n17
Kamchatka 74-5
Kampuchea *see* Cambodia
Kekkonen, Urho 93-4; *see also* Finland
Kennan, George 63
Kennedy, John F. 70
Khabarovsk 104

Index

Khmer Rouge 136
Khrushchev, Nikita 13, 19; domestic policies 9
Kishi, Nobusuke 62
Kissinger, Henry 98, 102
Korea 9, 21-2, 89-90; Demilitarized Zone 154; Korean War 34, 36-7, 52, 86-7, 147; North Korea 121, 137; *see also* Republic of Korea
Kosygin, Alexei 15, 93
Kuala Lumpur 135
Kuriles 104
Kuusinen, Otto 94; *see also* Finland

Laos 130, 144
least developed countries (LDCs) 138
Lebanon 132; *see also* Beirut
Libya 114
Lomé Convention 134, 150
Luxembourg 121, 135

MacArthur, Douglas 45
Macmillan, Harold 39
Malaya (Malaysia) 36, 89, 121, 135; *see also* Commonwealth
Manchuria 87
Marshall Plan 37, 85
Marx, Karl 140; Marxism 145
Mauroy, Pierre 38
Mediterranean 23, 58, 79
Metternich, Count 98
Mexico 121
Middle East 15, 90, 115, 123, 127, 146; and Soviet Union 58, 100, 131-2; and United States 66, 132; as source of energy 103, 117-19, 137; British military presence in 35; European peace initiative 163
Mitterand, François 38, 148
Mongolia 110, 131
Morocco 121
Mozambique 130-1, 134
Multilateral Force (MLF) 60
mutual and balanced force reductions negotiations (MBFR) 89
mutual assured destruction (MAD), doctrine of 16, 70, 77
MX ICBM programme 76

Napoleonic Wars 147
Nassau Agreement 40
Nasser, Gamal Abdul 9, 43, 143
NATO *see* Atlantic Alliance

Nehru, Jawaharlal 9, 143
Netherlands 123
New Zealand 79, 141
Nigeria 11, 49, 141, 143
Nixon, Richard M. 157; 'Basic Principles of US-Soviet Relations' (1972) 16, 30-1n15; 'Nixon Doctrine' (1969) 67; visit to China (1972) 65
Non-Proliferation Treaty (NPT) 14, 48, 89
Norway, 93, 123

Official Development Assistance (ODA) 122-4
Ohira, Masayoshi 135, 162
Ōkita, Saburo 134-5
Oman 136
Organization for Economic Co-operation and Development (OECD) 123, 151
Organization of Petroleum Exporting Countries (OPEC) 8, 10-11
Orwell, George 148
Osgood, Charles 155-6
Ottawa *see* summit meetings of industrialized states

Paasikivi, Juho 93-4; *see also* Finland
Pakistan 64, 124, 131, 146; and nuclear energy 18
Paris and London Agreements (1954) 59
Partial Test Ban Treaty 14, 89
Peaceful Uses of Outer Space Treaty 157
Pershing II 2, 60
Persian Empire 12, 145
Peru 121
Philippines 89, 121
Poland 28, 71, 76, 109, 131, 162; as source of coal 117; as source of refined copper 121; Soviet policy towards 84, 88, 98-9
Polaris 70
Porkkala 93
Portugal 126
Poseidon 73
Potsdam, conference of (1945) 45
Powell, Enoch 148-9
Pravda 85

Rambouillet *see* summit meetings of industrialized states
Rapallo, Treaty of (1922) 42, 53n15

Reagan, Ronald 102, 133;
　Administration 10, 66, 129; and
　arms sales to Taiwan 132-3,
　139n9; and public opinion 76,
　82n21; Inaugural Address 14,
　30n14; policy of sanctions 103;
　'zero option' initiative 76, 82n23
Red Sea 23
Republic of Korea 110, 121, 126;
　and nuclear energy 18; US
　military forces in 75; withdrawal
　of American forces 65; *see also*
　Korea; Rhee, Syngman
Rhee, Syngman 86
Roman Empire 12, 145
Romania 19, 84, 131
Russell, Bertrand 88
Russia *see* Soviet Union

Sakhalin 74-5, 104
Saudi Arabia 64
Schmidt, Helmut 10, 30n4, 109,
　135; policy over Pershing II and
　cruise missiles 60; relations with
　President Carter 66; speaks of
　Sarajevo 144; *see also* Enhanced
　Radiation Weapon, Federal
　Republic of Germany
Sea of Japan 23, 74, 104
Sea of Okhotsk 23, 74-5, 104
Second World War 8, 25
Servan-Schreiber, Jean-Jacques 149
Sierra Leone 121
Singapore 89, 126, 128; *see also*
　Commonwealth
Sino-Japanese Treaty of Peace and
　Friendship (1978) 104, 144
Sino-Soviet Treaty of Friendship,
　Alliance and Mutual Assistance
　(1950) 86
Six Days' War (1967) 15
Somalia 19, 144
Sonoda, Sunao 93
South Africa 11, 121, 144; and
　nuclear energy 18
Soviet Union: allied intervention
　after First World War 98; and
　central strategic balance 69-71;
　deterrence theory 13, 16-17;
　economic relations with Japan
　104-5, 112n27, 142; economic
　relation with Western Europe
　102-4, 142; economy 99; energy
　99-100; first nuclear explosion 9,
　38-9; military deployment in East
　Asia 74-5; military deployment in
　Europe 71-4; Orthodox Church
　140; Pacific Fleet 23, 74-5;
　population 99-101; Red Army
　37, 84-5, 93; relations with Third
　World 130-2, 136-7; security
　policy 23-4, 105-8; Siberia 101-2,
　103-4, 118, 141; Sputnik 9; *see
　also* Brezhnev, Leonid;
　Khrushchev, Nikita; Kosygin,
　Alexei
Spain 121, 126
SS-20, 2, 75, 78
Stalin, Josef 85, 87-8
Strait of Hormuz 118
Strait of Taiwan 19, 90
Straits of Tsushima 86
Strategic Arms Limitation Talks
　(SALT) 14, 65-6; and Poseidon
　73
Strategic Arms Reduction Talks
　(START) 76
Suez Canal 59; Anglo-French expedi-
　tion (1956) 43, 114
Sukarno 9
summit meetings of industrialized
　states 7, 79, 129, 143; Ottawa
　(1981) 147; Rambouillet (1975)
　79; Venice (1980) 79-80, 147
Supreme Allied Commander Europe
　(SACEUR) 59, 73-4, 154
Surinam 121
Suzuki, Zenkō 162
Sweden 93, 121, 123, 151
Switzerland 123, 150-1
Syria 131

Taiwan 126, 132-3, 139n9
Tehran 135; Conference (1943) 44
Thailand 121, 123
Thatcher, Margaret 40, 50; govern-
　ment 78
Theatre Nuclear Forces (TNF) 2,
　23; in Asian region 77-8
Thorn, Gaston 135
Tito, Joseph Broz 85, 135, 143
Treaty of Brussels (1948) 87
Treaty of Dunkirk (1947) 87
Treaty of Mutual Cooperation and
　Security between US and Japan
　(1960) 61-4, 78, 149, 172-5
Treaty of San Francisco (1951) 64
Trident 40

Index

Trilateral Commission 80
trilateralism 65, 128, 159
Tropic of Cancer 58
Truman, Harry S. 63
Turkey 121, 126, 146; and Atlantic Alliance 57, 71; economic assistance from Japan and German Federal Republic 124, 135
Tyumen oil field 104

United Kingdom *see* Britain
United Nations 158; Emergency Force 15; General Assembly 160; Security Council 7, 10, 15
United States: and central strategic balance 69-71; deterrence theory 13, 16-17; economic relations with Western Europe 37, 149; military deployment in East Asia 75, 154; military deployment in Europe 23-4, 71-4, 153-4; Official Development Assistance 122-3; relations with Third World 128-30, 132-3, 136-7; Seventh Fleet 75, 79; Sixth Fleet 79; Third Fleet 75; *see also* Acheson, Dean; Carter, Jimmy; Nixon, Richard M.; Reagan, Ronald
Urals, 2, 21, 38, 101

Venezuela 117
Venice *see* summit meetings of industrialized states
Versailles settlement (1919) 44
Vietnam 15, 56, 129, 133, 137; and Soviet Union 110, 131-2, 144-5; dominates Indochina 21; war 36, 67, 70

'War of Attrition' (1969-70) 15
Warsaw 89
Warsaw Pact 21, 134, 154; forces in Europe 71-4
Washington-Moscow Hot Line 15
Western European Union (WEU) 59
Wilson, Harold 60

Yakutia 104
Yalta Conference (1945) 19, 45
Yalu river 87
Yemen (south) 130-1
Yom Kippur War (1973) 15, 79
Yugoslavia 19, 130; expelled from Cominform 85

Zaire 114, 133
Zambia 121
Zhou Enlai 9
Zone of Peace, Freedom and Neutrality (ZOPFAN) 150